1968

Brazil's New Novel

FOUR NORTHEASTERN MASTERS

FRED P. ELLISON

Brazil's New Novel

FOUR NORTHEASTERN MASTERS

JOSÉ LINS DO REGO

JORGE AMADO

GRACILIANO RAMOS

RACHEL DE QUEIROZ

University of California Press

BERKELEY AND LOS ANGELES · 1954

UNIVERSITY OF CALIFORNIA PRESS
BERKELEY AND LOS ANGELES, CALIFORNIA

CAMBRIDGE UNIVERSITY PRESS
LONDON, ENGLAND

COPYRIGHT, 1954, BY
THE REGENTS OF THE UNIVERSITY OF CALIFORNIA

LIBRARY OF CONGRESS CATALOG CARD NUMBER: 54–11314

DESIGNED BY AMADEO R. TOMMASINI

PRINTED IN THE UNITED STATES OF AMERICA
BY THE UNIVERSITY OF CALIFORNIA PRESS

TO THE MEMORY OF
MY FATHER
LEE MONROE ELLISON

Foreword

BRAZILIAN LITERATURE *is little known in the United States. At long intervals an American critic may devote part of his activities to this rather exotic field. I am thinking of Isaac Goldberg and Samuel Putnam; others may translate important books from Brazil. Sometimes a Brazilian himself may come to the United States to tell Americans the wonders of his literature, as did Érico Veríssimo.*

All this is insufficient. Brazil has a vigorous and original literature, a literature that should be known abroad, not only as the revelation of the life of the country but as a body of outstanding works possessing a positive aesthetic value.

Some of these works have already appeared in English translations: Canaan, *by Graça Aranha;* Rebellion in the Backlands, *by Euclydes da Cunha;* Dom Casmurro *and* Epitaph of a Small Winner, *by Machado de Assis;* The Violent Land, *by Jorge Amado;* Anguish, *by Graciliano Ramos. Finally, that epoch-making book* The Masters and the Slaves, *by the great Brazilian sociologist Gilberto Freyre, was rendered into English. Even if brief, this is in fact an imposing and representative list of literary masterpieces.*

I would give the modern literature of Brazil a leading place

vii

in the literary production of Latin America. There are many prominent essayists, such as the sociologists Gilberto Freyre, Sérgio Buarque de Hollanda, Caio Prado Júnior; literary critics, such as Tristão de Athayde, Álvaro Lins, Lúcia Miguel Pereira, Mário de Andrade, Aurélio Buarque de Hollanda, Sérgio Milliet; there are great poets, such as Manuel Bandeira, Cecília Meireles, Murilo Mendes, Mário de Andrade, Augusto Frederico Schmidt, Jorge de Lima, Augusto Meyer, Carlos Drummond de Andrade, Vinícius de Morais, Mário Quintana; and excellent novelists: Lima Barreto, José Américo de Almeida, Mário de Andrade, Oswald de Andrade, Gastão Cruls, Lúcio Cardoso, Marques Rebêlo, Érico Veríssimo, Graciliano Ramos, Jorge Amado, José Lins do Rego, Rachel de Queiroz.

The last four, called the novelists of the Brazilian Northeast, constitute the theme of Mr. Fred Ellison's book. The choice reflects a commendable concern for literary quality. They are really the best from the standpoint of narration, stylistic capacity, psychological truth, emotional intensity, and social consciousness.

Mr. Ellison, led by his untiring devotion to Brazilian literature, and by his youthful enthusiasm, has given us the best interpretation of these four novelists. He presents them as a product of racial complexities, historical forces, and economic conditions: the writer in his milieu, man's interpretation of man, biological and spiritual factors in eternal struggle, society versus the individual. The picture is vivid, dramatic at times, always true to a reality which goes beneath the surface. More than a presentation of writers and their works, the present book is a genuine interpretation of a cultural process.

An interesting point to notice is the regional character of Brazilian literature. As an axiom we must accept "the regional" in Brazilian culture as a whole. It is evident, even today, that Brazil lacks unity, no matter from what angle we look at the problem. This fact may be lamented from a political standpoint, but, thinking of the enormous human variety in Brazil, the multiplicity of aspects, forms, and expressions, we must recognize the merits of this type of regionalism. Brazil offers the same picture as does the rest of Latin America: a number of regions thrown together by historical circumstances. In Brazil they constitute a nation; in Spanish America, a continent.

That in studying Brazilian literature a regional, rather than a chronological, criterion should be used seems to me the most logical line of approach. Mr. Ellison, in recognizing this fact, shows that elementary insight into a literary subject without which no profound understanding can be achieved. But he knows that "regional" does not imply an accumulation of irrelevant details, such as clothing, dances, cockfights, realistic landscape, vernacular language; to him, "regionalism" is the identification of man with a particular atmosphere: here, the man of Northeastern Brazil, as distinguished from the carioca *or the* gaúcho.

The intuitive approach has been implemented by technical devices and background references, thus completing a very sound critical attitude.

The bibliography of Latin American studies is enriched by this book, Mr. Ellison's first adventure in the world of belles-lettres. We hope that he will continue his work of interpretation of a culture so rich and yet so misunderstood in the rest of the world.

ARTURO TORRES-RIOSECO

Berkeley, California
March 15, 1954

Author's Preface

THE ORIGINAL *suggestion for this study of the new Brazilian novel stems from a literary poll conducted in 1941 by the* Revista Académica *of Rio de Janeiro. The event has since been widely publicized, and critics and literary figures of renown in Brazil have considered its results significant. One hundred eighty Brazilian writers were asked, "Who are the ten greatest novelists of Brazil?" The decision in favor of such luminaries of the past as Machado de Assis, Aluízio de Azevedo, Lima Barreto, Raul Pompéia, Manuel António de Almeida, and José de Alencar probably surprised no one. The outcome with respect to the four living authors selected by the critics was, however, of much greater interest. They were, in the order of relative prominence, Graciliano Ramos, José Lins do Rego, Jorge Amado, and Rachel de Queiroz. My own taste for Brazilian novels having been stimulated by the works of their predecessors, I decided to concentrate upon the four contemporary novelists and to present them as in every sense worthy of introduction to North American readers.*

Ramos, Lins do Rego, Amado, and Rachel de Queiroz actually have a great deal more in common than fine literary reputations and contemporaneousness. All happen to be natives of the Bra-

*zilian region called "the Northeast." They are not only com-
patriots but also associates and friends, although I am sorry to
report that one of them, perhaps the most distinguished Brazilian novelist of recent times, Graciliano Ramos, died on March
22, 1953. Their novels share so many characteristics that what
they have created must be viewed as an integrated regional manifestation. Analysis and evaluation of this phenomenon—surely
the most important literary phenomenon of the last twenty-five
years in Brazil—are the primary objectives of the present study.*

*Keeping in mind the poet Olavo Bilac's observation that
"Portuguese is the sepulcher of literature," which because of the
limited currency of the language must repose unread despite its
often magnificent artistic qualities, I have oriented my remarks
in the direction of, first, the general reader who does not know
Portuguese; second, the American admirer of Brazilian novels
through some of the good translations now appearing; and, third,
the student of Spanish literature in America who has not yet acquired proficiency in the sister tongue Portuguese. Throughout
the text, titles of novels as well as citations from them have been
translated into English. This orientation also accounts for the
detailed presentation of historical, political, and social background
for the novels.*

*Apart from the inspiration derived from the novels themselves,
which, read and reread, have never lost their appeal, I have received important encouragement from two friends, Professor
Arturo Torres-Rioseco and Professor Benjamin M. Woodbridge,
Jr., both of whom have communicated their enthusiasm and affection for Brazilian letters. It is a pleasure to express to them my
real sense of gratitude and obligation for whatever merits the book
may possess. I should also like to thank Miss Genevieve Rogers,
of the University of California Press, for generous editorial as-
sistance.*

*Grateful acknowledgment is made to the following publishers
for granting permission to quote from copyrighted materials:*

The Associated Publishers, Inc., The Negro in Brazil *(Washington, D.C., 1939), by Artur Ramos, translated by Richard Pattee; The John Day Company, Inc.*, The Brazilians, People of Tomorrow *(New York, 1947), by Hernane Tavares de Sá; Professor T. Lynn Smith, editor, with Alexander Marchant, of* Brazil: Portrait of Half a Continent *(copyright 1951 by The Dryden Press, Inc., New York, and reprinted by special permission); Alfred A. Knopf, Inc.*, Brazil: An Interpretation *(New York, 1945), by Gilberto Freyre; Alfred A. Knopf, Inc.*, The Masters and the Slaves *(New York, 1946), by Gilberto Freyre, translated by Samuel Putnam; The University of Chicago Press,* Rebellion in the Backlands *(Chicago, 1944), by Euclydes da Cunha, translated by Samuel Putnam; The University of Chicago Press,* Negroes in Brazil *(Chicago, 1942), by Donald Pierson; The University of North Carolina Press,* A History of Brazil *(Chapel Hill, N.C., 1939), by João Pandiá Calógeras, translated and edited by P. A. Martin.*

F. P. E.

Urbana, Illinois
April, 1954

Contents

I   INTRODUCTION   *Page*   3

II   JOSÉ LINS DO REGO   *Page*   45

III   JORGE AMADO   *Page*   83

IV   GRACILIANO RAMOS   *Page*   *111*

V   RACHEL DE QUEIROZ   *Page*   *135*

VI   THE NOVEL OF THE NORTHEAST   *Page*   *157*

NOTES   *Page*   *169*

BIBLIOGRAPHY   *Page*   *183*

INDEX   *Page*   *189*

CHAPTER I

INTRODUCTION

Introduction

THE BRAZILIAN literary capital at Rio de Janeiro
has been invaded and dominated in the last twenty-five years by
a little band of writers from a remote and now relatively minor
area, the far Northeast. To appreciate their disproportionate influence upon the intellectual life of Brazil, imagine, for purposes
of comparison, that the domain of fiction in the United States
were presided over by a group of writers from New England, an
area with which the Brazilian Northeast may well be compared
in cultural tradition and geographical situation.

Even better, compare the Brazilian Northeast with our own
Deep South, for in social, economic, and cultural pattern there is
a strong resemblance. Like the South, the Northeast was during
the colonial era the center of a rich agricultural economy based
not on cotton so much as on sugar cane, and its society was an
aristocracy of large landholders marshaling armies of slaves. On
these foundations arose a peculiarly stable culture which produced some of Brazil's greatest statesmen, scholars, artists, poets,
and novelists. Those who find in contemporary American literature a predominant number of leading novelists of Southern
extraction will see an interesting parallel in the Northeastern
novelists to be studied here. When the regional background is

3

understood, it seems less surprising that the Brazilian Northeast, set apart from the rest of Brazil by its colonial heritage and traditions, and now removed from the main stream of economic and political life, should still produce some of the most brilliant writers of the present age.

We might expect that the novel of the Northeast should bear the imprint of the regional culture and, in a broad sense of the word, be called "regional." Interestingly, regionalism is characteristic not only of the novel of the Northeast but also of virtually all Brazilian literature, especially the contemporary novel. Geographical, economic, historical, and cultural factors have had much to do with the partitioning in the output of modern literature. In an essay on this subject, Affonso Arinos de Mello Franco has indicated how the preëminence of sugar in the early colonial period made Pernambuco and Bahia the centers of defense of the Northeastern littoral; how the discovery of precious metals made Rio de Janeiro the political capital of Brazil; how the *bandeiras,* a regional movement centering about São Paulo, expanded the frontiers and increased the agricultural importance of the coffee-growing area; and how, finally, the new-found industrialism of that area is a regional phenomenon when viewed against the backdrop of Brazil as a whole.[1] Emphasizing the cultural diversity of the country corresponding to these different movements, Mello Franco concludes, "To deny that the Brazilian complex has reality only in the expression of its regional forces is to assume an attitude that goes against the indisputable evidence of our past and of our present."[2]

Logically, it has become common in recent years to approach the study of contemporary Brazilian literature with regional instead of purely chronological criteria.[3] A typical system of division is that of Érico Veríssimo, who identifies the following regions whose writers are individually contributing to a vast composite portrait of Brazil: the Amazon, the Northeast, Minas Gerais, Rio de Janeiro, São Paulo, and Rio Grande do Sul.[4] Each produces a distinctive literature. The novelist and critic Vianna Moog, in speaking of the "cultural island" of the Northeast, stresses the importance of such writers as Graciliano Ramos and José Lins do Rego. He sees the Northeast as a land of contrasts, the green of the tropical seaboard set off against the burnt brown of the arid *sertão,* the cities ever in contrast and conflict with the rural plantations, the Big House with the slave quarters, the rich with the poor, the white with the black, in this region of great racial diversity. And the critic adds, significantly, that this literature "could not but be a social literature, of society and of class . . . of plantation masters and of proletarians."[5]

Although the novelists of the Northeast are the chroniclers and interpreters of the region, their works are not to be looked upon as "regional" novels. The term, in Brazilian literature at least, is misleading, and too easily calls to mind the sentimental descriptions of the picturesque in the novels of the so-called "regionalists" of nineteenth-century Brazil. Therefore, although regionalism is an important aspect of the novel of the Northeast, the designation "regional" might well be avoided in referring to contemporary literature.

Americans are familiar with the so-called "bulge" of Brazil, the blunt upper corner, triangular in shape, that points squarely toward Africa. The Brazilians call this area *O Nordeste:* the states of Bahia, Sergipe, Alagoas, Pernambuco, Parahyba, Rio Grande do Norte, Ceará, and the coastal regions of Piauhy and Maranhão. Visualize this area as a colossal three-sided billiard rack, two sides of which represent the relatively narrow tropical belt which rims the coast. Within the rack, however, beyond the friendly littoral, lies the open sertão, which has characteristics so different that it is often called "the other Northeast."

The sertão is a land of calamity. Chroniclers have for several hundred years recorded its recurrent and protracted droughts, which may be followed by torrential rains. The scrawny vegetation may for a period of years die away to gaunt and tortured forms. With the first rains, the landscape revives, with nature seeking to repair the ravages of the *seca*. Physically, it is an area that cannot but tempt the novelist to re-create something of the drama of human life seeking to exist there. Our arid southwestern states with their spiny vegetation, vast lonely spaces, and undependable rainfall remind the Brazilian of the mysterious backland he calls the sertão.

The economy of the littoral, with its agricultural basis, is in sharp contrast with that of the backlands, which has since the sixteenth century been given over to grazing and, under certain conditions, to cotton. There are a few scattered towns, but the thin population is for the most part clustered about ranching headquarters. The *sertanejos,* or inhabitants of this wilderness area, are noted for their individualism, their ability to ride and herd, their superstitions, and their exaggerated sense of personal honor. Unlike our cowboys, they are not to be thought of as pioneers moving with a new frontier. Rather, as the geographer Preston James has said, they are a fragment of populations left over from the many groups that have sought to penetrate and exploit the riches of the interior.[8]

The novelists of the Northeast have often written of the sertão. Almost invariably, however, they have written as men from another world (exceptions are Graciliano Ramos and Rachel de Queiroz, who were reared in the sertão), from another civilization typified by the long-established plantations and towns along the coast. This was the land first seen by Portuguese explorers in the year 1500. Here, in the Northeast, was established one of the first successful colonies. When, in the middle of the sixteenth century, the Portuguese firmly organized their new holdings, colonial headquarters were set up at Salvador, or Bahia.

The Northeast, especially around Bahia and Recife, was the center of sugar-cane production. The crop is ideally suited to the fertile black or deep red soil called *massapé,* which forms the belt of agricultural land along most of the north-south coastline of the region. The tropical climate offers temperatures without extremes and throughout half the year plentiful rains.[7] This strip of territory resembles the Atlantic and Gulf coastal plain of the southeastern United States, where on great plantations a similar agricultural system was developed. The parallel of our Old South with the Northeast of Brazil is striking indeed. In both areas, after the Indians had been subdued, Negro slaves were imported, and a single crop came to predominate, forming the economic basis for a rural and aristocratic society founded on large landholdings and slavery.

One fundamental difference, however, is that miscegenation played no such role in the Southern states as it was to play in Brazil. The Portuguese, who have long been noted for their racial mobility, entered swiftly into the process of intermarriage. As Gilberto Freyre has pointed out, a people who had lived for centuries in contact with the Mohammedan conquerors of the Iberian Peninsula learned to respect not only their civilized accomplishments but also the Moorish idea of womanly beauty.[8] The Portuguese colonizer apparently had few prejudices against the copper-colored native woman, whose nudity was often enhanced by liberal applications of red paint. From the very start there was a mix-blood or mestizo population known as *mamelucos.*

The racial mixture of the African slave with the Portuguese has been symbolized in the title of Gilberto Freyre's *The Masters and the Slaves,* the English translation of *Casa-Grande e Senzala,*[9] which refers to the plantation manor house and its adjacent slave quarters. The author has documented in great detail the intimacy which characterized the relations between the *senhor de engenho* and his Negro servants. The mulatto offspring of these illicit but not unusual matings were to the masters like so much extra capital in an economic system based on slavery. In addition to the mulatto and the mameluco was the African-Indian mixture, or *cafuso.* Too much emphasis cannot be placed on the

racial composition of the Brazilian people and the social structure
typified by a feudal aristocracy with latifundiary estates worked
by slaves, for even today, despite the abolition of slavery more
than sixty years ago, the effects of the system are apparent. The
novelists of the Northeast, when they speak of contemporary
humanity, are usually dealing with the descendants of either
masters or slaves.

In the sixteenth, seventeenth, and early eighteenth centuries,
the Northeast, with its colonial capital at Bahia, was the intellectual center of Brazil. Education had begun to flourish in the
hands of the Jesuits, wealthy planters had made both Pernambuco
and Bahia centers of luxury and refinement, and it was not long
before men of leisure and culture were devoting themselves to a
literature whose predominant theme was the beauty and wonder
of Brazil.[10]

The splendor of Bahia and the importance of the Northeast
were destined to fade when, in the late seventeenth century, gold
was discovered far to the south. Never since, except in the realm
of culture, has the region regained its prominence; the transfer
of the colonial capital to Rio de Janeiro signalized its lost hegem-
ony. Early in the nineteenth century, when John VI, fleeing
Napoleon, passed over Bahia in preference to Rio de Janeiro as
the seat of his freshly transferred government, its secondary role
in government was settled. During the empire, the Northeastern
senhores de engenho were the mainstays of the regime of the
magnificent scholar-emperor Dom Pedro II. These aristocrats,
however, had begun to witness the dissolution of their cherished
social and economic structure. The Brazilian South, with coffee,
came into its own. Foreign competition in sugar hurt the Northeast's main stock in trade. Restrictions on the slave traffic tended
to favor the coffeegrowers of the São Paulo area, and finally, when
Dom Pedro's daughter decreed the emancipation of all slaves
without compensation to their owners, an economic collapse en-
sued. A year later Dom Pedro II was forced to abdicate, and a
republic was established in 1889.

The Northeast, too far from the center of government, has continued to languish in comparison with sections that are geographically and economically more favored. In recent years big sugar refineries have superseded many small mills, causing further disintegration of the social order. Small properties have had to be consolidated to provide the cane needed to sate the ever encroaching *usina,* or sugar refinery. Absentee ownership of land has multiplied difficulties, and the drought recurs periodically. Other problems—disease, poverty, and illiteracy—are not native to the Northeast, but have found a propitious place in which to grow more acute.[11]

If the Northeast has had to step aside for the more affluent areas to the south, it has nevertheless maintained its cultural prominence, nurturing generation after generation of writers who have enriched Brazilian literature. Some of the most important are the internationally known religious orator of colonial times, Padre António Vieira; the seventeenth-century satirical poet Gregório de Matos; the nineteenth-century poets Castro Alves and Gonçalves Dias; the novelists José de Alencar, Aluízio de Azevedo, and Domingos Olympio; the positivist philosopher Tobias Barreto; the critic Sylvio Romero; and the statesmen and essayists Joaquim Nabuco and Ruy Barbosa.

This historical background of literary excellence is one of the important reasons for the flowering of novelists of the Northeast in the 1930's. Their profound cultural traditions are undoubtedly the product of a social system which until fairly recent times had unusual stability. Several Brazilian critics, among them Werneck Sodré, have pointed out that the present literary upsurge is connected with the ancient pattern:

The economy based on sugar cane, which for so long dominated one zone of the country, formed a characteristic mentality. Ever stable, the system has a past and a long tradition that became solidified. It is able to produce, upon the sensibility of the sons of the regions where it held sway and where it extends even today, a lasting impression. Its stable outlines are projected in time.[12]

Sérgio Milliet, the *paulista* sociologist and critic, has contrasted the stable culture of the sugar-cane areas with the intensely mobile culture associated with coffee in the São Paulo region. He concludes that "civilization arose from a permanent culture."[13]

The recent literary activity among the *nordestinos* is explained best by the sociologist and social historian Gilberto Freyre, himself a Northeasterner, who has said that the diseased culture of the Northeast "makes us think of the oysters which give pearls."[14] The novels of the Northeast are a handful of those pearls.

The history of the Brazilian novel of the Northeast is not complete without mention of a writer who, paradoxically, was neither a nordestino nor a novelist. Euclydes da Cunha, from the old province of Rio de Janeiro, is the author of a work translated into English as *Rebellion in the Backlands (Os Sertões)*,[15] which has had a heavy impact upon present-day novels of social content. The book's literary significance has been well stated by Samuel Putnam, its translator:

> *Rebellion in the Backlands* may be said to have posed the problem which faces the twentieth-century novelist of Brazil: that of how to achieve an artistic synthesis of the rich social content which his country affords him. Because he grappled with this problem so valiantly and solved it in so extraordinary and individual a fashion, the author continues to be a symbol and an inspiration to creative writers. It is surely not without significance that there has grown up in this same general region, the Northeast, a school of novelists—Jorge Amado, Graciliano Ramos, José Lins do Rego, to mention but a few—who are this moment bringing new life to Brazilian letters, and whose influence on the national literary scene has been so profound as to constitute something very like an "invasion."[16]

Rebellion in the Backlands, which Euclydes wrote for a São Paulo newspaper, is his report of the so-called Canudos campaign by federal troops in the sertão of northern Bahia. It describes the four expeditions sent by the government in 1896–1897 to capture or kill one António Maciel, a mentally deranged individual who wandered the sertão and was thought to perform miracles. "António the Counselor," as he was called, was lifted on a wave of primitive religious fanaticism to become the spiritual as well as temporal leader of a motley horde of sertanejos. Promising them Heaven and defying the newly established authority of the republic, he led his several hundred followers to a deserted cattle *fazenda* at Canudos. It required thousands of well-equipped soldiers, after serious reverses, to wipe out António and his indomitable *jagunços,* or backlands outlaws.

The author adopts, as nearly as possible, a scientific approach, with chapters on history, anthropology, geology, and geography, as well as on-the-scenes reporting. If the book is not properly a novel and defies classification according to any literary genre,[17] stylistically it is unique. Euclydes has transformed a report which might have been read by a few hundred specialists, at most, into something imposing. Observation and research have been coupled with the liveliest sort of imagination—here rests the book's claim to be regarded as art and not merely as *reportage* or scholarship. After setting forth the details, the author draws conclusions concerning the larger meaning of what he has seen. To express his grandiose visions, he often uses a Latinizing form of expression peculiarly his own, heroic in movement and noble in tone. The style frequently presents difficulties even to Brazilians, but, as Samuel Putnam has observed, it is "as rugged as the sertão itself"[18] and seems altogether appropriate to the author's magnificent narrative.

Euclydes da Cunha's intention was to shock Brazil to its senses, to make its people understand that the tragic incident at Canudos was the fault of the entire nation, which had allowed the sertanejos to live like ignorant and superstitious savages along the margins of civilization. "The entire campaign would be a crime, a futile and a barbarous one, if we were not to take advantage of the paths opened by the artillery, by following up our cannon with a constant, stubborn, and persistent campaign of education, with the object of drawing these rude and backward fellow-countrymen of ours into the current of our times and our own national life."[19]

Probably the most important consequence of Euclydes' report was the controversy it aroused. The shameful debacle at Canudos symbolized the grave internal weaknesses with which the new republic would have to contend. Euclydes gave warning that the so-called civilized communities of the seaboard must integrate the backward but courageous sertanejos into national life.

Because *Rebellion in the Backlands* is a book of high literary quality, it has never ceased to circulate or to remind the nation that it must seek to remedy the serious and widespread ills that still exist. Euclydes da Cunha has helped to draw the attention of Brazilian scholars and scientists away from Europe to their own culture and society. Above all, he has helped to create a climate of self-knowledge and self-criticism, without which the novel of the 'thirties, the novel of the Northeast, might never have been written.

José Lins do Rego, reflecting a contemporary view, considers *Rebellion in the Backlands* "our first great regionalist work, much more of the land than the novels of Alencar. . . . His book is great because of the contact it establishes between the public and a piece of Brazil."[20]

In proposing the integration of the sertanejo in the national life, Euclydes raised a delicate issue which still preoccupies the thoughtful Brazilian, the question of race. He was pessimistic about the "degenerate" mestizo,

lacking the physical energy of his savage ancestors and without the intellectual elevation of his ancestors on the other side. In contrast to the fecundity which he happens to possess, he shows an extraordinary moral hybridism: a brilliant mind at times, but unstable, restless, inconstant, flaring one moment and the next moment extinguished, a victim of the fatality of biologic laws, weighted down to the lower plane of the less favored race.[21]

Gilberto Freyre, in a recent work, pointed out that Euclydes was the victim of "ethnocentric exaggerations," widely held in Brazil at the turn of the century, which stemmed from too rigid an adherence to the views of certain nineteenth-century investigators of race: Gobineau, Vacher de Lapouge, Weismann, and others.[22] Although he did subscribe to such views, Euclydes nevertheless admired the fierce jagunços.

An antidote to the prevailing lack of confidence in the Brazilian mix blood was given in 1917 by a then rather obscure sociologist, Alberto Torres, in *The Problem of Brazilian Nationality (O Problema Nacional Brasileiro)*.[23] Though highly optimistic about grave political, economic, and social problems, the book met with indifference and was almost forgotten until recent times. Brazilians now consider Alberto Torres to be one of their most eminent twentieth-century thinkers; Gilberto Freyre has called him "an older brother of our generation."[24] Availing himself of the findings of the American anthropologist Franz Boas, Torres stoutly combated the pseudoscientific notion that the Brazilian people are inferior because of mixed ethnic strains.

Notwithstanding the present-day investigations by such scientists as Gilberto Freyre, Artur Ramos, Roquette Pinto, and Edison Carneiro, who have generally borne out Torres' conclusions, Brazilians often appear unconvinced of the soundness of their racial make-up. In fact, the student of Brazilian history in the first three decades of the present century may at times get the impression that the whole country is suffering from an inferiority complex. Writers attempted to represent Brazil as the rustic *caboclo* "Jeca Tatú, squatting on his haunches, silently 'calculatin'," or as an "immense hospital," or as "a refined piece of Africa," to mention only a few of countless unflattering comparisons.

Brazilians were, at any rate, more willing to look squarely at reality, not with blind optimism, but seeing both the good and the bad in the Brazilian scene. The findings of investigators have not always been pleasant: the grinding poverty among a large segment of the population, with attendant deterioration in food, clothing, and shelter, the lack of sanitation and the consequent high incidence of disease, the poor system of transportation, the widespread illiteracy, and a multitude of other ills.

Three distinct but related developments of the 'twenties in Brazil were revolutionary in character. A dramatic political rebellion, starting in 1922, prepared the terrain for full-scale revolution. In the same year the movement called "modernism"—an upheaval in the arts—got under way.[25] And soon thereafter began the so-called "traditionalist, regional" movement of the Brazilian Northeast. A turbulent but fecund period, the 'twenties are better understood in the light of historical developments.

The new republic had been unstable from the outset because of differences between civilian and military factions. And, like many other Latin American republics, Brazil had too slavishly imitated the governmental organization and liberal constitution of the United States. The result was a malfunctioning of the process of representative government. Years of dictatorship and civil strife were interspersed with periods of peaceful progress. In the second and third decades of the twentieth century, militarism and political "bossism" proved to be almost catastrophic, particularly when complications resulting from the economic dislocations of the First World War were felt in Brazil.[26]

In 1922, a critical year for both literature and politics, a Northeasterner, Epitácio Pessoa, held the presidency of the nation. He was under attack for having appointed civilians, contrary to custom, as heads of the two branches of the military service. A military revolt erupted against the government. Merely an angry spark, it was soon put out, and some historians have been willing to dismiss it as a political maneuver to defeat the civilian candidate Artur da Silva Bernardes in the presidential election of 1922.[27] Many others discover in the rebellion a deeper significance: the expression by a small but courageous group of army officers, for the most part *tenentes,* or lieutenants, of a new variety of political idealism.

That the men who died in this rebellion were idealists can easily be seen from the facts surrounding this curious incident. It began on July 5, 1922, when elements of the army at the Military School and at the forts of Leme and Copacabana—the latter overlooking the lovely beaches where even then Brazilians were at play—rebelled against the government. Loyal troops ordered out by Pessoa immediately crushed the rebels, with the exception of those at the fortress of Copacabana.[28] For three weeks the garrison, with about a hundred men and officers, held out against thousands of besiegers. Then it was decided to dismiss all troops who cared to surrender, and to attack the encircling forces with the remaining officers and men.

These numbered only seventeen, and they were joined by one civilian who, happening by, shouldered a rifle when he learned the objective of the march—"To our death, to help save Brazil," as one of the rebels is reported to have said.[29] The Brazilian flag that had flown over the fortress was divided into eighteen pieces and now, each wearing a piece of that flag over his heart, they quixotically charged the thousands of troops entrenched along Copacabana beach. Machine-gun fire finished sixteen of them. Two officers, Siqueira Campos and Eduardo Gomes, though gravely wounded, survived to become leaders of the 1930 revolution.

The political party of these two and of others like them came to be known later as the Lieutenants' party (*partido dos Tenentes*) and was destined to play a decisive role in the early phases of the revolution of 1930. What had motivated the now consecrated eighteen men? A contemporary writer has set forth his conception:

They had no specific political program, and rendered tribute to no particular political ideology. Indeed they were not politically minded, nor did they have a program of action. Theirs was a naïve idealism that refused to accept passively the atmosphere of apathy, corruption, and pettiness under which successive republican administrations were smothering the country.[30]

There was much in Brazilian social and political life against which the citizens might complain. In the early years of the republic, constitutional guaranties of personal liberties had often been suspended. Elections, which Euclydes da Cunha once characterized as "a euphemism which with us is the most striking instance to be found of the daring misuse of language,"[31] frequently served the interests of the landowning aristocracy. The chief executive was all-powerful and, when it suited him, intervened in the affairs of the states; the states themselves were often under the control of *caudilhos,* or petty barons. Any president could virtually name his successor: the states of Minas Gerais and São Paulo, with but two exceptions, had alternated in furnishing the chief of state.

The dramatic protest of the Copacabana rebels was echoed by the Lieutenants and others during the 'twenties, for conditions became increasingly bad. The entire administration of President Bernardes, who succeeded Pessoa in 1922, has fittingly been described as one of "politico-military intrigue and revolutionary ferment."[32] On July 5, 1924, a far more serious revolt occurred in São Paulo, where elements of the army rose against the government. The choice of the second anniversary of Copacabana leaves no doubt that this movement springs out of the earlier uprising.

At this juncture Luis Carlos Prestes enters Brazilian history. To this day his long shadow lies across the path of his country. In April, 1925, the young officer, who had distinguished himself at the Military School, welded the revolutionaries from São Paulo and from the state of Rio Grande do Sul into what is now called the "Prestes Column." Sharing his command with Miguel Costa, Prestes got rid of dissidents and, departing from the jungle state of Paraná with fifteen hundred men, plunged into the endless Brazilian interior on one of the most remarkable military undertakings in Latin American history. The purpose seems to have been to evade the pursuing federal forces and to prolong the revolution. Afoot and on horseback the Prestes Column in two years covered thousands of miles through the most difficult and varied terrain, across jungles, swamps, mountains, sertões, and river barriers, from the southernmost corner of Brazil to the states of the Northeast.[33] Hundreds of battles were fought with pursuing armies. Finally, exhausted but undefeated, the column escaped into exile in Bolivia early in 1927.

In modern Brazilian history the Prestes Column has a significance far beyond the military and strategic aspects of the daring exploit. For two years the revolutionary spirit of the Lieutenants was kept glowing as Prestes attempted to carry his political and social revolution to the backward people of the interior. Prestes himself is quoted, in a statement made in 1928, in regard to his revolutionary aims: "What we had in mind principally was to awaken the populations of the interior, drawing them out of the apathy in which they were so submerged, indifferent to the fate of their country, hopeless of any remedy for their ills and sufferings. An undertaking of a political and social character . . ."[34] Prestes appealed to these neglected people, especially the rural workers, for support of his project of social reform. They, along with urban workers, constituted a new force in Brazilian political life. To the distressed and illiterate masses Prestes became the "Knight of Hope," as some have called him. In fairness it must be pointed out that no specific political doctrine animated the Prestes Column; it was not until after the march that its leader became a convert to Marxism, living in Russia and serving as an official of the Executive Committee of the Communist International.[35]

The Prestes Column with its "revolution in being" was not the only outbreak of the mid-twenties; others occurred in the states of Amazonas, Pará, Parahyba, and Pernambuco and in the capital at Rio de Janeiro.[36] None succeeded, and there is no evidence that Prestes' forces actively took part in these fruitless rebellions. They all, nevertheless, were indicative of the precarious state of the body politic. This is the period of the establishment of Brazil's Communist party, of the growth of Marxist and other leftist political agitation, of strikes, and of popular dissatisfaction.

Does a revolutionary leader like Luis Carlos Prestes have any real connection with literature? At least one contemporary writer, the novelist Jorge Amado, whose partisanship may well be kept in mind, thinks so.

No one compared to him has had a greater importance, a more decisive importance. Modern Brazilian literature, that part of it which has produced the great social novels, the sociological studies, the rehabilitation of the Negro, the historical studies, is a direct result of the cycle of revolutions begun in '22 and extending even to this day; [the revolutions of] '22, '24, '26, '30, and '35 gave the people a part to play, interesting them in the problems of Brazil and giving them a desire for knowledge, from which there arises the present literary movement. And since Luis Carlos Prestes was and is the central figure of all these movements, their chief, guide, and general, his connection with modern Brazilian literature is undeniable.[37]

Although Amado's estimate of the significance of Prestes is somewhat exaggerated, it is useful testimony to the relation between art and political life.

Critics have not hesitated to associate intimately the artistic and military events of 1922. Oswald de Andrade declared: "Modern Art Week . . . can never be separated from the uprising at the Copacabana Fortress. Both happenings were to do no less than signal Brazil's majority."[38] Another critic explains their connection thus: "It was a common anxiousness for renovation, in the limitless field of art and on the vast horizons of Brazilian society and politics. These two movements, apparently dissociated, had their roots joined in the depths of the same earth. It was the same consciousness which was being freed by the force of the pen and of the sword."[39] The parallel development of a political revolution and a literary movement which surely deserves to be called a revolution profoundly affected the entirety of Brazilian artistic life—music, painting, sculpture, and especially literature.

Modernism is usually said to have begun with the so-called

Modern Art Week in São Paulo, where, on February 13, 1922, a group of young intellectuals sponsored an exhibition of cubist and expressionist plastic arts, along with concerts of modern music and readings of poetry by members of the group.[40] Guilherme de Almeida, Ronald de Carvalho, and Mário de Andrade read poems in the new manner. The first night, with its hullabaloo of cheers for the new examples of artistic expression, and protests against them, recalls the Battle of *Hernani* nearly a hundred years earlier in Paris, when Victor Hugo's new play in a new manner won a startling victory.

The modernists in literature had begun to smash the Parnassian and Symbolist molds that had long been accepted in Brazilian poetry. Mário de Andrade, the "pope of modernism," as he was playfully called, states that "the modernist spirit and its modes of manifestation were directly imported from Europe."[41] After the First World War, numbers of Brazilian intellectuals had gone to Europe, where some of them had come under the influence of men like Cocteau, Picasso, Tristan Tzara, and Marinetti, who headed vanguardist movements in art and literature.[42] Inspired by these iconoclasts, it is no wonder the early Brazilian *modernistas* devoted themselves to destructiveness and often to what the Brazilians call *cabotinismo,* or clowning. This aspect of the movement is well illustrated by the first important creation of modernism, Mário de Andrade's *Hallucinated City (Paulicéia Desvairada*), in which the poet, with singular freedom and good humor, depicts his own fresh view of life in São Paulo.

Like its political counterpart, the revolutionary modernist movement enlarged its sphere of action and influence as the decade progressed. The original nucleus, mostly of poets, was headed by Mário de Andrade and Oswald de Andrade in São Paulo. By 1924 some of the best poets in other localities had caught the new spirit, men of the caliber of Manuel Bandeira, Carlos Drummond de Andrade, Ribeiro Couto, and Álvaro Moreyra. A widely publicized event in connection with the new cause was the speech delivered in 1924 before the Brazilian Academy of Letters by Graça Aranha, a venerable novelist who had lent his support and prestige, although he had little to do with originating the movement.[43] In a challenging statement, he accused the Academy of standing in the way of progress in Brazilian letters.[44] He then made a dramatic exit from the chambers on the shoulders of ecstatic young admirers, and soon thereafter resigned from the august body.

After its opening fireworks, the modernist movement entered a more positive and constructive phase. An important collection of poetry on Brazilian themes by Oswald de Andrade shows, even in its title, *Brazilwood (Pau Brasil),*[45] the new preoccupation with things Brazilian, which is perhaps the most noteworthy single aspect of modernism. The work contains a manifesto of the poet's intention to know his country better and to sing of it, not in the language of Camões but in something much closer to the Brazilian vernacular. Other works containing *brasilidade,* as the tendency toward literary nationalism was sometimes called, are Ascenso Ferreira's *Country Man (Catimbó)* and Raul Bopp's *Negro Drums (Urucungo).* Jorge de Lima's *That Negress Fulô (Essa Negra Fulô)* is probably the finest of all the poems reflecting the modernists' interest in the cultural contribution of the Negro to Brazilian life. Another major achievement was Bopp's *The Snake Norato (Cobra Norato),* with a theme of the Amazon basin from Indian mythology.

The chief importance of these nativist poems is their emphasis on national folklore, their attempt to plumb the national psychology, and their influence upon modern novelists to treat Brazilian themes, regions, and peoples in preference to more cosmopolitan subjects. This last point was exactly what Euclydes da Cunha had taught his generation to do at the turn of the century; his presence pervades modernism as well. As an investigator of the movement has observed, "There seems to be a clear relationship between the thought of Euclydes da Cunha and the content of modernism."[46] The best critic of modernism, Alceu Amoroso Lima, refers to the nativist tendencies of the movement as the literary "incorporation of everyday reality."[47] An equally important characteristic of modernism, as discerned by Amoroso Lima, is described as "the freeing of verbal forms." This is particularly important in the study of the novel.

A single Brazilian modernist, Mário de Andrade, and a single work, his *Macunaíma: The Hero without Any Character* (*Macunaíma: O Herói sem Nenhum Carácter*), published in 1928, must form the basis for any study of the modernists' influence upon the literary language. The book has been called a *chanson de geste* of Brazilian folklore. Its hero is a Brazilian Tyll Eulenspiegel who romps playfully through the land and represents "young Brazil, the astute but unlettered heir to all the cultures, all the instincts, and all the customs and music of the most ancient races."[48] No work in the country's literature has given so comprehensive a view of the diverse aspects of Brazilian life, including the vigorous and colorful language which Brazilians speak and which, up to that time, had rarely found its way into print.

Actually, the language of *Macunaíma* is a linguistic tour de force, being "composed of all the idioms and all the vocabulary of all the particular dialects of all the localities of Brazil, combined arbitrarily."[49] Mário de Andrade included many a passage unintelligible even to Brazilians, but his aim was to communicate the national mode of speech and psychology synthetically. In his desire to renovate the literary language, he even went to the point of creating an artificial gibberish that was academic, not popular, in conception.[50] However, many a writer of the 'twenties later imitated the poet-philologer, if not in his calculated exaggerations, certainly in his aim to approximate contemporary Portuguese in all its lexical and syntactical peculiarities.

Concerned mostly with poetry, modernism has influenced nearly every phase of literature, and above all the novel of the Northeast. "A rare phenomenon," says the Portuguese critic

José Osório de Oliveira, "that in modern Brazilian literature poetry opened the way for the novel."[51] We cannot agree with some Brazilian observers that the novel of the Northeast is solely the creature of modernism. Neither can we deny that there is a connection between the literary ferment of the 'twenties and the subsequent social novel. The truth lies somewhere in the middle. Modernism, with its introspective interest in Brazil and its constructive innovations in the literary language, broadly channeled the course of the new fiction in the Northeast as elsewhere in the nation.

It is much simpler to document the influence of another intellectual force working upon the new novel. The traditionalist regional movement in the Northeast got under way in 1923, when Gilberto Freyre returned to his native Pernambuco. Glimpsing anew the old city of Recife with its fragrant cashew trees, ancient churches, and dilapidated streets, he saw a Pernambuco that others did not see.[52] Through his delightful articles on regional life, his searching interpretation of the social scene, and his prose style of ingratiating naturalness and unusual lyric quality, Freyre made his compatriots see all this. He showed the catalytic activity for which he is justly famous, first, by gathering collaborators for a *Book of the Northeast* (*Livro do Nordeste, 1925*), a little-known work on many aspects of life in the region,[53] and second, by the organization of the first regional congress to be held in Brazil,[54] getting together in a common creative effort people of the most divergent tendencies—the governor of the state, the archbishop, priests, judges, senhores de engenho, lawyers, doctors, old Negro cooks. From the first, Freyre gave impetus and orientation to the regional movement, one of the most fruitful and artistic undertakings in the country's history: he was its inspirer, its leader, its philosopher.

In one way we of the United States may share a bit of Freyre's glory, for this son of once affluent sugar planters of Pernambuco studied in our universities, principally in Columbia University, and was strongly impressed by American scholars, particularly by the anthropologist Franz Boas. Even then the serious young Brazilian (only eighteen at the end of the First World War) was preoccupied with the destinies of Brazil. As a Brazilian, he was concerned about the problem of miscegenation. He tells of having once seen a group of Brazilian sailors—mulattoes and cafusos— crossing Brooklyn Bridge and of their having struck him as caricatures of men. With a certain distress he recalled a phrase written by an American traveler in Brazil: "the fearfully mongrel aspect of the population." "This," thought Freyre, "is where miscegenation leads."[55]

But from his anthropological studies with Boas he began to understand the true worth of the Negro and the mix blood and to formulate one of the central ideas, perhaps *the* central idea of his entire work: there is a fundamental difference between *race* and *culture* and we must learn "to discriminate between the effects of purely genetic relationships and those resulting from social influences, the cultural heritage, and the milieu."[56] Henceforward Freyre devoted himself to a study of the race, culture, and society of his homeland; all his preliminary investigations and writings contributed to his monumental study of Brazilian civilization, *The Masters and the Slaves*.

This book truly marked an epoch: Brazilians today speak of their intellectual life "before and after *The Masters and the Slaves*."[57] Never before had they been able to understand so much about their past, their present, and their potentialities. As a social philosopher, Gilberto Freyre has led his fellow countrymen to see the Portuguese colonizer, the Negro, the Indian, and the mix blood in a new light. And in endeavoring to demonstrate that the fusion of races and cultures in Brazil has produced new, important, and desirable values in their society, he has helped to modify the national inferiority complex. As an individual, his personal qualities and example have "influenced decisively an entire generation of Brazilians."[58]

Freyre's influence now reaches well beyond the confines of his region, and he is the best-known figure among Brazilian thinkers —so well known that he is called simply "Gilberto," a tribute the people reserve for those in the public domain. Measured by its impact upon thoughtful men up and down the coasts of Brazil, Freyre's own work must rank as the most significant achievement of the traditionalist regional movement.

This movement was, like modernism, a reaction to what Freyre has called "narrow colonialism," a blind subservience to European values and standards. The modernistas were anxious to forget, even to obliterate, the past, in their desire to create a fresh Brazilian literature. As one of them has stated, they would gladly have consented to the destruction of the ancient towns of Olinda, Ouro Preto, or Bahia "in the name of what we supposed to be modern Brazilian culture."[59] The group headed by Freyre in Pernambuco would, on the contrary, accept what was valuable out of their European heritage, and at the same time try to discover a new set of values "in harmony with the tropical landscape and with Brazilian conditions of life."[60]

Both modernism and traditionalist regionalism were reactions against "the conventions of classicism, of academicism, and of Lusitanian purism."[61] Each sought independently to bring the literary language closer to the spoken. Freyre and his group discovered "profound affinities" with some of the modernists whom Freyre met in Rio de Janeiro and São Paulo—Manuel Bandeira, Prudente de Morais Neto, Rodrigo Mello Franco de Andrade, Carlos Drummond de Andrade, Affonso Arinos de Mello Franco, and others who shared his interest in Luso-Brazilian folklore, the Indian, the Negro, and the mestizo.

Freyre has said that the two movements, the modernist school of the South and the group which he headed in the Northeast, "will probably stand as the most significant in revolutionizing the letters and the life of Brazil in the direction of intellectual or cultural spontaneity, creativeness, and self-confidence set against the tradition of colonial subordination to Europe or the United States."[62] In affirming the existence of two important intellectual trends in the 'twenties, leaving aside the political, Freyre makes clear that he is independent of the modernists. At the same time, with a careful gesture he includes in his own group the novelist José Américo de Almeida, the forerunner of the novelists of the Northeast. We are thereby to understand that much of the credit for originating the nordestino novel in 1928 goes to the traditionalist regional movement.

Only now, a quarter of a century later, can the vitality of the nordestino movement be properly assessed. Apart from the extensive writings of Gilberto Freyre himself, Brazilian scholarship has been enriched by investigations of society and culture by some of his compatriots, in ethnology, sociology, history, architecture, and art. Painters influenced by the movement are Cícero Dias, Manuel Bandeira (not to be confused with the poet of the same name), and Luis Jardim. The last-named is also a contemporary master of the short story; some of his works, indelibly regional, are among the finest of this genre in Brazilian literature.

Literary criticism is well represented by Sylvio Rabello, Olívio Montenegro, and above all by Álvaro Lins, who, though still a young man, is perhaps the most brilliant literary critic of Brazil today. The most important novelists associated with the traditionalist regional movement are José Lins do Rego and José Américo de Almeida.[63]

José Américo de Almeida belongs to a literary type fairly common in Latin America but seldom seen in our United States— the writer who is at the same time a distinguished public official. During the 'twenties he was a lieutenant of the Parahyban governor, the later martyred João Pessoa, who was then engaged in organizing, with Getúlio Vargas and others, a powerful new political group, the Liberal Alliance. This group contained elements of the Lieutenants' party which prolonged some of the idealism of the Copacabana rebels. When the revolution exploded in 1930, the novelist Américo was one of its leaders. In the early 'thirties he was a cabinet member in the first revolutionary government of Vargas and later came near being President of Brazil. Now, in the 1950's, after having been governor of his state, he is back at his old job of Minister of Public Works and Transportation in the newly reëlected Vargas administration. Politics has indeed circumscribed the literary career of this long-beloved public figure.

Political ends helped shape Américo's first major work, *Parahyba and Its Problems* (*A Parahyba e Seus Problemas*), a vast sociological treatise with a message of social reform, dedicated to Epitácio Pessoa, the first national president to be elected from the Northeast. The work, which is of interest because it serves as a key to the three subsequent novels of Américo, takes up the geography, geology, history, economics, anthropology, and social organization of the state of Parahyba. Here and there the study shows a true scientific spirit, with conscientious documentation of major affirmations. Elsewhere, however, the author makes an impassioned defense of his main thesis: that Parahyba has been abandoned by the rest of Brazil to suffer cataclysms of drought and of consequent social and economic disorganization.[64] He argued that if federal funds were advanced to build dams, roads, wells, and other improvements, the area might well become a land of plenty, a veritable new Canaan. Through such expedients most of the grave social problems of the region—poverty, ill health, prostitution, crime, and illiteracy—would be quickly solved.

The most absorbing part of the book, that entitled "Social Consequences," gives a clear insight into the human problems arising from the catastrophe of drought. Américo offers first-hand observations on basic social and ethnic types, the *praieiro,* the *matuto,* and the *vaqueiro,* the inhabitants of the beach area, the fertile agricultural zone, and the pastoral sertão, respectively. He contrasts the agricultural region with the arid plains and crags of the backlands, where grazing and cotton hold sway.

The ugly antagonism between the society of the backlands and that of the coast, the lack of social solidarity between sertanejo and matuto, are the central themes. Reflecting a modern point of view, Américo broaches the problem of *mestiçagem*, or miscegenation, without pessimism in regard to the mestizo. In fact, he combats the racialist views of Gobineau, citing such Brazilian authorities as Alberto Torres on the possibilities of the man of the Northeast.[65]

José Américo reveals a community of interest with his friend Gilberto Freyre, whose findings he anticipated in a limited way in studying the social structure of the agricultural belt with its Big House and near-by slave huts.

No writer, however, has influenced Américo half so much as Euclydes da Cunha. In its often scientific point of view, in its conception and treatment of major social problems, Américo's sociological work is clearly modeled upon *Rebellion in the Backlands*. The author makes frequent references to his predecessor's work in setting forth several aspects of his study of Parahyba, whose backland regions, or sertões, are very similar to those of the state of Bahia, which Euclydes described. The impression of kinship is strengthened by the language in which Américo delineates life in the Northeast, with the same emotive power and striking imagery found in *Rebellion in the Backlands*. Euclydes may well have been the strongest influence upon the subsequent novelistic style of Américo, although the modernist renovation of the literary language also may have left its mark.

At the time of the appearance of Américo's first and most significant novel, *Cane-Trash* (the translation of the title *A Bagaceira* was suggested by Samuel Putnam), the novel as a genre had been overshadowed by poetry. The few novels produced by the modernists, for example, Mário de Andrade's *Macunaíma* (if this curious work can be called a novel), reflected an experimental tendency and were significant mostly for innovations in language. It is true that some of the older novelists, men like Gustavo Barroso, Afrânio Peixoto, and Xavier Marques,[66] had carried on in the nineteenth-century tradition of depicting manners in conventional regional settings. But there is no evidence to indicate that these waning novelists exerted the slightest influence upon such novels as *Cane-Trash*.

The novel takes its name from the Portuguese *bagaceira,* or place where the bagasse (cane pulp) is stored after the grinding of the sugar cane. By extension the word may refer to the area where the sugar mill grinds the cane and, by further extension, to the whole "moral atmosphere of the sugar-cane mills."[67] Américo refers to "cane-trash" in the latter sense, and Putnam's translation of the title suggests the moral dissolution of the individual.

Into such an atmosphere the novelist introduces a group of Brazilian Joads, sertanejos driven from their home country by the drought. Here is his vision of the *retirantes,* or refugees, as they at last reach the well-watered plantation zone:

> It was the exodus from the drought of 1898. A resurrection of ancient cemeteries—skeletons back from the dead, with the smell and the earth-quality of putrid graves.
> The mutilated phantoms moved as if dancing, so crippled were they, and unsteady, at the dragging pace of those who carry their legs instead of being carried by them.
> They walked slowly, looking backward, as if they wished to return. They made no haste to arrive, because they did not know their destination. Driven by swords of fire out of their paradise, they wandered aimlessly at the whim of an evil fortune.
> They fled the sun and the sun led them in their forced nomadism.
> Emaciated to the point of comicalness, they kept growing larger, as if the wind were blowing them. And their hands shook on shrivelling arms which hung down to their knees.[68]

The sertanejos are given work on the plantation. Their near-slavery, the traditional submission to the authority of the patriarchal senhor de engenho, contrasts strikingly with the freedom once enjoyed on the open ranges of the sertão, where the ranchers had hardened into a race of proud and independent people.

The conflict between the modes of life of the "two North-easts" is the principal theme of *Cane-Trash*. Lúcio, son of the planter Dagoberto, but at outs with his father because of his broader education, falls in love with the wild and tempting Sole-dade, only daughter of the sertanejo refugee Valentim. A variant of the Oedipus situation is present when Dagoberto deflowers the girl, winning her away from his son. Meanwhile Valentim murders one of Dagoberto's men in a vain attempt to protect the virtue of his daughter, who willingly becomes the mistress of the senhor de engenho. The scene then shifts to the sertão, where Dagoberto is killed in an accident and Soledade is left for dead after a fight. Later, a high point of the novel is Valentim's de-fense by the lawyer Lúcio. The old sertanejo is acquitted.

Through him, Américo attributes much of the misery and mis-fortune to the drought, which cast Soledade and her family into the noxious atmosphere of the bagaceira. For the downfall of the girl the author, through his *raisonneur,* the lawyer Lúcio, blames the bagaceira—the lasciviousness of the patriarchal senhor; the promiscuity of the workers, who live in ignorance, filth, misery; and the tropical plantation atmosphere where men and women, particularly the women, fall to earth like ripe fruit to putrefy.

The novel ends with a postscript and a preachment. Seventeen years after the events related, during the drought of 1915, Soledade returns to the green littoral after having been given up for dead. Lúcio welcomes her and the child—his own half-brother—to the plantation where he has sought to carry out social reforms, par-ticularly of the bagaceira. The workers, however, grudgingly ac-cept the drought-stricken sertanejos who accompany Soledade. The enlightened planter must decry what still exists despite his attempted reforms: the lack of racial solidarity between sertanejos and matutos, who still behave like natural enemies. As one of the characters remarks, not even their dogs could get along to-gether.

An undisputed merit of the novel is its breadth of sociological

scope, its synthesis of the salient aspects of life, both in the littoral
and the sertão, into a moving story. And in Soledade, Américo
has created an unforgettable character, the incarnation of feminine attractiveness. She has certain traditional sertanejo characteristics too. Her father's misfortune, her responsibility for it, her
fall into another social level akin to prostitution, she accepts almost passively, with the backlander's resignation. She seems particularly convincing when, untamed and primitively passionate,
she seeks to avenge her lover Dagoberto. What the seca may do
to this beauty and fire is part of the tragedy unfolded in the closing pages.

The major weakness of the novel lies in its literary form. As
Andrade Muricy has observed, there is a regrettable lack of correspondence between the observed reality of characters and actions
and the language in which this reality is projected.[69] An exception may be made for much of the dialogue, in which the author
has sought to capture the essence of popular speech. The human
events upon which the novel is based are ugly and somber, but
the novelist's descriptions of them are intensely poetic, with too
much imagery, too much striving for effect: "Soledade represented
all the trials of the drought. She no longer kept even that accent
of withered beauty to be found in some romantic apparition.
Deathly dark circles extended around her eyes like a violaceous
face mask. Over her long frame her blackened skin was wrinkled.
And her cheeks were so sunken that she seemed to have three
mouths."[70] Obviously, Américo was trying to convey his vision
as artistically as possible, but the result is artificiality. Subsequent
writers of the Northeast learned to let their expression arise
naturally from the theme.

The favorable reception given to *Cane-Trash* was due in no
small part to the prevailing state of mind in the late 'twenties:
critics were willing to acclaim a well-written thesis novel, probably because most thinking Brazilians were acutely concerned

with social and political problems. Reading Américo's book today, we may be less inclined to respond to appeals that are no longer compelling.

Although he is by no means the most gifted of the Northeastern novelists, Américo is a key figure in the development of the recent novel. Rarely does the literary investigator come upon a writer who so well epitomizes an era. He was prominent in two of the three main currents of the 'twenties. In the cultural sphere he was among the first, with Freyre's traditional regionalists, to find the artistic inspiration latent in the Northeastern scene. He appears to have been only marginally in contact with the literary rebellion called modernism,[11] but in politics, where demands were mounting for reforms in national life, he helped carry the pathetic idealism of the Copacabana rebels into a new revolutionary phase.

Forces had been accumulating in Brazilian life since the Copacabana rebellion in the early 'twenties. When the economic crisis of 1929 struck Brazil, coffee was the first commodity to be affected and soon thereafter other phases of the economy dependent upon it. Millions of Brazilians were forced to an even lower level of subsistence, thereby lighting the fuse of revolution.

In the federal government, President Washington Luis, from the state of São Paulo, played into the hands of the revolutionaries when, just before the election of 1930, he designated another paulista, Júlio Prestes, to be the conservative party candidate for the presidency. It was not so much his arrogance in choosing to appoint his successor as his decision to go against the traditional alternation in office between the two powerhouse states of São Paulo and Minas Gerais that precipitated trouble.

Political leaders of Minas Gerais entered into the so-called Liberal Alliance with opposition forces from other states. Getúlio Vargas had won the support of many of the Lieutenants, or tenentes, who were now famous as officers of the Prestes Column.

But the chief himself, Luis Carlos Prestes, had recently joined the Communists and, from his exile in Montevideo and Buenos Aires, was actively opposing the movement led by Vargas, on the ground that the working classes were not well represented.[72]

In the presidential election in March, 1930, the Liberal Alliance candidate was apparently defeated by the conservative Júlio Prestes (not to be confused with Luis Carlos Prestes), but the losers refused to accept the results. Intrigue was in the air and, on October 3, 1930, the military phase of the revolt began. Gaining control of civilian and military establishments in the state of Rio Grande do Sul, the rebels, headed by Vargas, began an armed march on the capital. Resistance was slight, and in only one month—this is called the October rebellion—the *gaúchos* from the South completed their coup by taking over the government in Rio de Janeiro.[73] Dissolving the congress and suspending constitutional guaranties, Vargas decreed absolute powers for himself and his government.

As a reformer, and in answer to widespread public demands, Vargas immediately announced plans affecting many phases of Brazilian life: he would improve public education, welfare, and health; he would create a Ministry of Labor; he would gradually reduce large landholdings; and he would seek a more diversified agriculture. José Américo de Almeida, as Minister of Public Works and Transportation, began to execute his dream of defeating the weather in the drought area of the Northeast.[74]

However, other problems won priority in the early years of the new administration. In 1932 a full-scale civil war—a prominent historian has called it "one of the most serious revolts in the entire history of Brazil"[75]—had to be fought against the wealthiest and most populous state, São Paulo. Though defeated, the paulistas achieved one of their goals when Vargas granted them amnesty and agreed to convoke a constituent assembly. The constitution of 1934 offered hope for the solution of weighty social and economic problems. However, a new trend became apparent when in 1934 Américo quit his cabinet post to protest Vargas' compromise with the large financial interests of his country, as well as with certain foreign governments anxious to exploit the resources of Brazil.[76] It could be seen that the liberal Lieutenants' party was withdrawing the support that had helped bring Vargas to power.

Despite presidential promises, the standard of living of both rural and urban workers was still low, and they were being awakened to a new class-consciousness by radical organizers. The strike had become a political weapon. Moreover, the Communist party, founded in Brazil in the early 'twenties, had grown stronger and now posed the threat of an even more drastic revolution. And to counterbalance the left came a threat from the right: the rabidly nationalistic and fiercely anticommunist *Integralista* party under the leadership of Plínio Salgado, another literary figure with civic aspirations. This avowedly fascist group was instrumental in spreading the propaganda of the German and Italian governments, which had begun to exert an appreciable influence upon certain elements in Brazilian life.

Early in 1935 Luis Carlos Prestes, the "Knight of Hope" of the celebrated march through the Brazilian interior, returned to Rio de Janeiro after a sojourn in Russia. He was to head the National Liberation Alliance (*Aliança Nacional Libertadora*), an ultraradical political movement which was just getting under way in various parts of the country and soon gained a large popular following.[77] On July 5 (the anniversary, significantly, of the Copacabana uprising) Prestes announced the aims of the new party: "cancellation and disavowal of foreign debts," "abrogation of unpatriotic treaties with imperialism," "nationalization of the most important public services and of imperialist enterprises not subordinated to the laws of government," "satisfaction of the needs of the proletariat," and "distribution among the poor population, whether rural or urban, of lands and water rights, without indemnity to imperialists, or to reactionary large landholders, including the Church."[78]

All the established institutions were under attack. There is good reason to believe that the Alliance was, in its leadership at least, Communist-inspired. It has been so described by more than one contemporary historian. Even when the leaders of the Alliance were forced underground, after Vargas outlawed the party on July 11, 1935, the movement did not lose its vitality.[79] Late in November a rebellion broke out in the state of Rio Grande do Norte and, two days later, in Recife. Immediately, Prestes, as leader of the movement, ordered part of an infantry regiment and the cadets at the School of Aviation in Rio de Janeiro to extend the revolution to the capital.[80] The outbreak there, however, was crushed in less than a day, and the entire revolutionary movement collapsed.

After the abortive coup, the Communists and other leaders of the National Liberation Alliance were hunted down relentlessly. All Brazil was clamped under martial law. A reign of terror began and lasted through 1936.[81] The historian P. A. Martin thus describes the aftermath:

First and last nearly 10,000 arrests were made, including some 6,000 in Rio alone. Among the prisoners were a number of university professors, the prefect of the Federal District (an eminent physician by the name of Pedro Ernesto Batista), Senator Chermont, several deputies, and other persons of prominence and distinction. Though the spokesmen of the government insisted that communism was the sole cause of the insurrection, the opinion was general that the government feared hostile opinion and that the causes of the unrest lay far deeper than the grievances of certain extremists in the rank and file of the army.[82]

The Alliance was utterly crushed when its leader, Luis Carlos Prestes, who had been in hiding, was surprised and seized. He was held incommunicado for almost ten years, until the Vargas regime was retired.[83]

In the early period of the revolution, before the dictatorship, "Brazilian culture awoke upon a new life."[84] It was as if the energies released to overthrow the old order were also sufficient to produce a renaissance in the arts, particularly in literature: poetry, the essay, and the novel began to flourish as never before in the nation's history. And in this new period of revolutionary enthusiasm, achievement, and promise, politics and literature became even more closely interrelated than in the 'twenties.

Because the novel of the Northeast is predominantly social and sociological, it could not but respond in its early phase to the same forces then shaping political history. No literary creation was ever more the product of its times. The critical spirit so keen in Euclydes da Cunha thirty years earlier was now revived by many thoughtful Brazilians, especially by the modern novelists. Paralleling the popular desire for reform reflected in the demands made upon the government of Getúlio Vargas, there was a profound literary preoccupation with the problems of Brazil. The novelists broached them in a sober and realistic manner. Not only was there a chorus of social protest but also, in this era of extreme partisanship, an out-and-out political orientation in some novelistic writing. More than ever before, the novel focused upon the wretchedness of the lower classes. The resulting new psychological insight into character is surely one of the lasting gains attributable to the new literature, particularly to that of the Northeast.

Why should the novel of the Northeast have become the predominant literary force in the early 'thirties? The answer seems to be that the novelists of that region were most attuned to the spirit of the times. Many of them could write of social issues with conviction and from experience.

Actually, it was necessary to document the intolerable conditions in the various parts of the nation. Some Brazilians, taking uncommon pride in their land, in the generosity of nature, and secure in the belief that "nobody dies of hunger in Brazil," were unaware of the serious situation in the Northeast and in other parts of the country. "Many city-dwellers still believed in the idyllic life of the country, as if the illiterate and worm-eaten caboclos were shepherds out of Vergil."[85] "What one saw were scenes of misery, the futile struggle of man against his environment, against abandonment by the authorities, religious superstition, political chicanery, social injustice, economic depression—a sad and somber picture."[86]

The Northeastern novel of proletarian leanings was at first accused of "vulgarly repeating life"[87] or was stigmatized as a "sociologizing novel,"[88] especially by critics in the South. The opinion of Sérgio Milliet, one of the most perceptive of paulista critics, is representative: "Despite their vigor, the Northeasterners brought to Brazilian literature a monotonous and inexorable atmosphere of permanent misfortune, which in no way corresponded to the mentality and interests of São Paulo. With pretensions to a social literature, they viewed all problems through a prism that was not ours and thereby made them frequently incomprehensible in our eyes."[89]

The Southern region, center of modernism in the 'twenties, had to relinquish its literary preëminence to the nordestinos in the 'thirties. "The axis of the Brazilian novel has suddenly shifted from South to North. There has been an unexpected movement of decentralization, a chance movement, subconscious and unforeseen, but very significant. All at once the North began to send to Rio novels that no one had counted on. The critics were obliged to recognize them."[90]

Eloquent testimony to the vitality of the novel of the Northeast is given in an essay written by Sérgio Milliet a few years later. Explaining how his own feelings had changed, Milliet says that, although the São Paulo critics maintained their opposition to the proletarian novel, they were at last won over to the rich social theme of the Northeast. They became aware that the problems of the Northeast, as revealed in the novels, were an index of the weaknesses in the entire social structure of Brazil. In the words of Milliet, "Since that moment when, through the works of the nordestinos, we saw our own rustic caboclo—our own tormented common denominator—we have begun to take advantage of their lesson."[91]

By the mid-thirties the Northeasterners had won acceptance throughout Brazil with novels some of which are works of art as well as social documents. José Américo de Almeida had shown the flight of the retirantes, or refugees, from the drought areas. Rachel de Queiroz followed in 1930 with *The Year Fifteen (O Quinze)*, a story with a similar setting, and, two years later, *John Michael (João Miguel)*, dealing with the inmates of a little jail in the backlands. Amando Fontes, in *The Corumba Family (Os Corumbas)*, showed the distintegration of a farm family in an industrial city of the Northeast.

The theme of the Northeast was given new dignity and breadth with the appearance of *Plantation Lad (Menino de Engenho)*, in which José Lins do Rego began his magnificent survey of the decline of the sugar-cane aristocracy of Parahyba. Also in the early 'thirties came the debut of Graciliano Ramos, who had seen the tragic consequences of cyclic drought in the sertão, the breakdown in the long-established patterns of society. *Caetés* (the name of an Indian tribe) describes the monotony of small-town life in the interior of Alagoas; *St. Bernard (São Bernardo)*, the fight over possession of an agricultural fazenda. Jorge Amado told of the exploitation of workers in southern Bahia in *Cacao (Cacáu)*, and of the horrors of slum life in the city of Bahia, in *Sweat (Suor)*.

In particular, 1935 was a year of brilliant flowering. Three novels about the Northeast appeared at that time: in *The Whirlpool (Calunga)* Jorge de Lima dwelt upon human decadence on a malaria-infested island off the coast of Alagoas; and José Américo de Almeida resumed novelistic activity with *The Hide-Out (Coiteiros)*, on banditry, and *The Notch (O Boqueirão)*, on the conflict between old and new at the scene of an engineering project in Parahyba.

What was the fate of Brazilian writers during the martial-law era brought on by Prestes' rebellion in 1935? In that year Gilberto Freyre, certainly a moderate in matters political, was arrested in Recife and fingerprinted as an "agitator" when he signed a manifesto against one of the repressive measures of the Vargas regime. Two years later he was set upon by henchmen of the federal *interventor* of Recife and obliged to defend himself by main strength.[92] In the same period, because of opinions expressed in *The Masters and the Slaves,* he was attacked in print by "members of the Jesuit wing of Catholicism, one of whom demanded for *The Masters and the Slaves* the extreme punishment of an auto-da-fé, insisting that both the book and its author be burned."[93]

Jorge Amado was imprisoned and his works were subjected to scrutiny; the security police arrested two other prominent novelists, the gaúcho Dionélio Machado and Graciliano Ramos. The latter was transported to Rio from his native Alagoas on mysterious charges, and was imprisoned for several months at a penal colony.[94] While there as a political prisoner, Ramos, already one of the most respected of Latin American novelists, contracted tuberculosis as a result of his incarceration.

After 1936 Brazil appeared to be returning to the quieter paths of constitutional government. National elections were in the offing and Vargas had promised to give the candidates a free hand in appealing to the people. One of the candidates, the novelist José Américo de Almeida, represented the liberal position. The others were a former governor of São Paulo, a spokesman for powerful business interests in the South; and Plínio Salgado, the leader of the green-shirted, fascist-aping Integralistas. The German and Italian press, no doubt with *Lebensraum* in view, threw their support to the Integralistas, after Vargas himself repudiated the European fascists. The party of Américo attracted an immense following, but attempts were made to discredit it as Communist-controlled. The candidacy of the paulista was jeopardized when one of his supporters was suspected of plotting revolution on his own.[95] The two latter factions failed to merge forces and, in fact, tended to cancel out each other's chances for victory. It looked as if Plínio Salgado might win.

So it looked, at any rate, to President Vargas. On November 10, 1937, he staged a *coup d'état* by promulgating a new constitution which "declared a national emergency, dispensed with the national legislative body, and authorized the president to govern the country by decree."[96] Four days later he outlawed the Integralistas and abolished the elections. To all intents and purposes, Getúlio Vargas, once the head of the democratic and popular revolution of 1930, was now the dictator of Brazil. The new constitution through which he functioned was very different in character from the liberal-spirited documents of 1891 and 1934. In one important respect, the provision for a national economic council to coördinate the economy, the constitution of 1937 bore a strong resemblance to that of the corporative state in Italy.

Probably the most noteworthy innovation of the Vargas "New State" (*Estado Novo*) in its impact upon the cultural life of the country was the setting up of a Department of Press and Propaganda (*Departamento de Imprensa e Propaganda*—"D.I.P."), which controlled and censored all forms of communication; a decree-law of December 27, 1939, gave the agency the right to restrict the entry into Brazil of "foreign publications harmful to Brazilian interests, and to forbid, within the national territory, the publication of those which may offend or impair the good repute of the country, its institutions or its morals."[97] This is the so-called "Law of Literature," for infractions of which authors, editors, printers, and vendors were held accountable. The D.I.P. made clear its opposition to "so-called proletarian literature," whose aim was to "promote intellectual disorder," and publishers were alerted against such "immoral literature."[98] The D.I.P. also declared that the development of Brazilian culture was to be characterized by the patronage and intervention of the New State in matters of art, literature, and education.[99]

During the dictatorship of Vargas, personal liberties were curtailed. Repressive measures were taken against many private citizens, particularly those who failed to conform, as was more than once true of certain writers of the Northeast. The gallant Freyre was often under physical surveillance, his correspondence was violated, and as late as 1942 he again suffered physical attack in Recife, because of an article he wrote denouncing Nazi activities in the port.[100] During this period Jorge Amado spent much time in exile, and José Lins do Rego on one occasion was constrained to lead a delegation of writers to the dictator to assure him of their "loyalty."[101]

To what extent did political events after 1935 account for the perceptible shift in literary direction among the novelists of the Northeast? The tendency may best be noted in the partial relinquishment of social themes in favor of psychological studies, the soft-pedaling of political propaganda, and for certain authors a complete silence. Jorge Amado laid down his pen, as did Graciliano Ramos and Rachel de Queiroz.[102] All three were avowed enemies of the dictatorship. Of the nordestino writers only José Lins do Rego kept up his novelistic activity throughout the Vargas regime.[103] In 1936 there was a noticeable decline in creative writing of all kinds.[104]

The late Samuel Putnam was convinced that because of restrictions and suppressions the Brazilian writers of the late 'thirties had to "trim their sails" in order to produce books that could be sold. He found Jorge Amado abandoning the proletarian novel as a consequence of political events.[105] But did Amado actually abandon the novels dealing with lower-class heroes engaged in political and social struggle? It would rather appear that he gave a more artistic form to the proletarian novel. As late as 1937, Amado continued to convey a political message. After 1937, however, he ceased to write until 1943, when he published *The Violent Land* (*Terras do Sem Fim*). Significantly, the political note is missing. This work is universally held to be his best, often on the grounds that in it he did not seek to make propaganda. How ironic that his political enemies should thus be indirectly responsible for Amado's most artistic accomplishment!

Graciliano Ramos was stifled by the oppressive atmosphere of dictatorship to a greater degree than the other Northeastern novelists. While he was still in prison his *Anguish (Angústia)* was published in 1936. Its chief novelty lies in the adaptation of the so-called interior monologue to the needs of the psychological novel. Samuel Putnam believed that Ramos' resort to this Joycean technique was a kind of disguise, "for Getúlio Vargas is not likely to object to a 'complex,' to the interior monologue, or the analysis of a Lady Chatterley as endangering the stability of his regime."[106] As another kind of subterfuge, according to Putnam, Ramos "has had to muddy his language at times almost to the point of unintelligibility, knowing that the prison gates are always there, threatening to close on him once more."[107]

Putnam may be correct in his assertion that there is a cause-and-effect relation between the dictatorship and the novel. But he may have failed to understand that, with the possible exception of Ramos' first book, the novelist is preoccupied with the social theme of Northeastern society. Usually, however, Ramos treats this theme in connection with the psychological study of an individual. What Putnam takes for a "disguise" of the novelist's true feelings is rather an ingenious method of combining the social with the psychological. This is no subterfuge but rather an example of Ramos' artistry. Nowhere does he make his attitude toward society unequivocal. It is therefore unthinkable that he could have, as Putnam suggests, "muddied his language" in order to deceive the censors.

In 1938 Ramos carried on the social theme with *Parched Lives (Vidas Secas)*. He wrote no more novels, and from the early 'forties until his recent death produced only a handful of short stories and one important volume of memoirs.[108]

Rachel de Queiroz departed from the sociological theme of her first two novels in *Stony Road (Caminho de Pedras,* 1937). It is true that some of the central figures are Marxists and radical labor agitators, but in no sense is this a novel of political hue; the labor movement merely provides the background for the central psychological study. In *Three Marias* (*As Três Marias*, 1939) even the political background disappears as the author proceeds with her psychological analysis of feminine character. It augurs well for Brazilian literature that Rachel de Queiroz, after twelve years of silence, recently began publication, in serial form, of a new novel, *The Golden Cockerel* (*O Galo de Ouro*).[109]

Lins do Rego, in *Purity* (*Pureza*) and *Fresh-Water Creek* (*Riacho Doce*), relegated the sociological aspects of his novels to an inferior position, concentrating upon a sexual theme of aberrant personalities. *Wondrous Rock* (*Pedra Bonita*), however, is an important social novel in the line of descent from *Rebellion in the Backlands*. We cannot agree with Samuel Putnam that *Wondrous Rock* is a departure from the broad social themes of the Sugar-Cane Cycle and a return to "the picturesqueness and exoticism of the old regional romance and short story: to the blood-drenched religious fanaticism, the brigandage, and the exacerbated sensuality of the hinterland."[110]

Lins do Rego's twelfth novel, *The Bandits* (*Cangaceiros*),[111] after being published in serial form, has just appeared as a book.

Thanks to these writers, the novel of the Northeast, a literary phenomenon of the 1930's, has continued to hold a respected position not only in the 'forties but in the 'fifties as well. "A literary freeze" is what one Brazilian critic calls the present situation of the novel, and he notes that even now "Brazilian literature is living off the force of a literary movement that burst upon the country in 1928."[112] From the year of José Américo's *Cane-Trash* until the present, the novel of the Northeast—characterized by its interest in man in his regional environment, by its implicit (and sometimes explicit) note of social protest, and by its endeavor to discover psychological truths in man, no matter what his walk of life—has represented an important cultural value of modern Brazil.

CHAPTER II

JOSÉ LINS DO REGO

José Lins do Rego

JOSÉ LINS DO REGO is himself the "plantation lad" of his well-known Sugar-Cane Cycle of novels. Particularly in his early writings, he relies upon a prodigious memory for the events that he sets down, often in the form of memoirs. But his books are also wrought of an imagination that lifts mere recollection to the level of art. Although it is not easy to unravel the facts of his life from the fiction of his work, some details are available to increase our understanding of the novels.

The novelist was born on June 3, 1901, the descendant of an aristocratic planter family that has been established for hundreds of years in the agricultural zone of southern Parahyba. His mother, Dona Amélia Lins, died a few months after his birth, and his grief-stricken father, João do Rego Cavalcanti, retired to his plantation, leaving the boy in the care of his aunts and maternal grandfather, José Lins Cavalcanti de Albuquerque, in whose Big House he was born.[1] The domain of his grandfather's sugar plantation included nine engenhos scattered along the *várzea,* or bottom lands, of the Parahyba River, from the Atlantic Ocean westward to the edge of the sertão. "Corredor" (the plantations were named, as were our own Hermitages or Monticellos),

45

in the novels of the Sugar-Cane Cycle, became the "Santa-Rosa" of the plantation lad Carlos de Mello.

Modeled upon the master of Corredor and dominating the first three novels of the cycle is "that saint of a sugar-cane planter," Colonel José Paulino.[2] His daughter, the fictitious Maria-Menina, who until her marriage is a second mother to Carlos de Mello, is probably a composite of two of José Lins do Rego's aunts, Tia Maria and Tia Naninha, who cared for the boy in the first ten years of his life.[3] The family portrait of many another figure from actual life is drawn in these novels; sometimes Lins do Rego casts his relatives in a novel without even bothering to change their names!

Many episodes are based upon actual experiences—the great flood of the Parahyba River, Carlos' contact with exuberant nature as he roamed wild about the plantation, his visits with his aunt to the homes of tenants and other plantation workers. An experience on which Lins do Rego based an entire novel was his early schooling at the Institute of Our Lady of Carmo, at Itabaiana, where the tender personality of the future novelist was to a degree shaped by the disciplinarian Eugénio Lauro Maciel Monteiro, the famous Maciel of the novel *Daffy Boy*.

The childhood of the novelist was anything but normal. In many respects Lins do Rego is the sickly Carlos de Mello, called "Daffy Boy" because of his moodiness (and because his father was in an insane asylum—a fictitious note, it would seem). Dependable testimony comes from Olívio Montenegro, who has known the novelist well and reveals the temperament of the author as a boy. In his opinion, Lins do Rego was "a creature different from the rest, a difficult child, one of those whose wishes never know firm ground, and who seem always to be fluctuating between the earth and the moon . . ."[4] As an impulsive and precocious child he, like his creation Carlos de Mello, sought release from his troubles in flights of the imagination and in juvenile attempts at writing.

When he was eighteen years old, Lins do Rego entered the School of Law in Recife, where, during four years of preparation, he was to open a serious breach between himself and his plantation background. This was a time of important influences. Lins made the acquaintance of José Américo de Almeida, an older man he greatly admired for personal and intellectual qualities. He was also fortunate in his friendship with Olívio Montenegro, a man of cultured and critical tastes who steered the young law student in the direction of Balzac, Stendhal, and Dickens.[5]

The greatest day in his artistic life, however, came in 1923, when he met Gilberto Freyre in Recife. "From that moment to this," says Lins do Rego, "my life has been different, my thoughts have been different, my plans, my readings, my enthusiasms."[6] Freyre, with his cultural background, orderly mind, and elegant manner, was everything that Lins do Rego was not, and the latter confesses that he began to imitate Gilberto in all things, even in literary style. It was Gilberto who gave him his first lessons in English, who introduced him to Joyce, Maritain, Ganivet, Pater, Browning, and others. Freyre scoffed at the excesses of the modernists of the day, and it may have been because of him that Lins do Rego never aligned himself with the movement.[7]

Lins do Rego once took Gilberto Freyre, a city man, to visit the moist green plantations of Parahyba, his people of the engenhos, the old family servants, the workers in the fields, where the cane waved in the bottom lands that had been the haunts of his boyhood. Curiously, he feared that Gilberto, who was engrossed in studying the planter civilization represented by his people, might be disappointed in what he saw. This anxiety seems to betray the fact that Lins himself, after having broken nearly all ties with his plantation past—in exactly the same way as did Carlos de Mello in *The Old Plantation*—had not yet become reconciled to his old way of life.

Gilberto was to show him the way home again. Perhaps on such a trip, in the company of one who had a profound under-

standing of the culture of the Northeast, Lins do Rego may have
learned to venerate the grand traditions of his native land. Perhaps the novelist-to-be grasped the fact that he himself had un-
suspectingly played a part in a tragic act of Brazilian history,
when the patriarchs of a brilliant old civilization were toppled
and there were no more to replace them. Lins do Rego is the
first to acknowledge the decisive influence of the author of *The
Masters and the Slaves:* "I write about him, and I speak almost
of myself, so much do I feel myself to be his creation, so great
was the influence that he exerted upon my poor abilities . . ."[8] The
fact that these words were written in retrospect, after both men
had become renowned, may account for their nostalgic quality.

Lins do Rego, in the middle 'twenties, was prosecuting at-
torney in a hamlet in Minas Gerais, and later a bank inspector in
Maceió, the capital of Alagoas. Devoting his leisure to literary
affairs, he in turn began to influence others, with some success,
if we may judge from the circle of admiring young writers who
surrounded him: Valdemar Cavalcanti, Aurélio Buarque de
Hollanda, and others. "I owe them a great deal," says the novelist,
"for the encouragement, the interest, and the warmth with which
they aided me in writing my first novels."[9] Maceió was, in the
late 'twenties and early 'thirties, if not the literary capital of the
Northeast, certainly the spawning ground of most of the major
writers of the region. Its literary circle included Graciliano Ramos,
Rachel de Queiroz, and, for a time, Jorge Amado. In an environment highly favorable to "cross-fertilization of thought," little
wonder that José Lins do Rego remembers the Alagoan phase of
his life as "a fecund time, the period of the burgeoning of my
career."[10]

In 1930, when the revolution began, the fledgling novelist
found himself allied with persons who were by nature counter-
revolutionary. He lost his government job to the Vargas-led in-
surgents, and it was only through the intervention of his friend
José Américo de Almeida that he was able to regain it. What a

strain the revolution must have placed upon the loyalties of Lins do Rego! A son of the old regime and a man of apparently conservative tastes, his thinking nonetheless seems to have been in tune with that of many of the new spirits, such as José Américo, who cried for change.

Lins do Rego's first novel, in 1932, reveals his deep sympathy for the ordinary people. This solidarity with the lowly, perhaps shown best in *Black Boy Richard,* is found in nearly all his novels. Although he was active during the 'thirties in campaigning for social reform, he stated his convictions in the form of the essay,[11] and has kept his novels free from demagoguery.

When, in the mid-thirties, Lins do Rego was transferred in his position to Rio de Janeiro, his literary reputation was already firmly established. His first two novels were soon printed in second editions. He was active also as a *cronista,* or contributor of articles to newspapers and reviews, and as a translator of English, Spanish, and French works, employing a veritable bureau of literary reporters and stenographers.[12] His interests, which he is fond of sharing in print, include sports, politics, music, art, motion pictures, and science, especially medicine, a considerable knowledge of which he has acquired through being a confirmed hypochondriac—a clue, perhaps, to the psychology of the fictional Carlos de Mello!

Those who know José Lins do Rego invariably emphasize those qualities that make him "the eternal *menino de engenho":* his drawling, high-pitched voice of the Northeasterner, his capricious syntax and use of odd survivals of Portuguese forms unknown in the rest of Brazil. And they speak of his eccentricities, his love for practical jokes, his habit of playfully hurling obscenities at his friends in public—some, indeed, think that the semiautobiographical "Daffy Boy" was well named. But there is also the silent, preoccupied Lins do Rego who seems to be feeding upon his melancholy—the facet of the novelist's temperament which is most easily identified with that of the fictitious Carlos de Mello.

Whether they see him as a sensual madcap (a figure of their Mardi Gras) or sad as only they themselves can be, Brazilians are inevitably attracted to Lins do Rego and his books. His peculiar combination of the highs and lows in the national makeup may account for the late Mário de Andrade's dictum to the effect that in Brazilian artistic creation he recognized only three masters: Heitor Villa-Lobos, Cândido Portinari, and José Lins do Rego. A fair inference from this opinion by the author of *Macunaíma* is that Lins do Rego is to modern literature what Villa-Lobos is to music, what Portinari is to painting. He does resemble them in forcefulness, individualism, tropical fecundity: in inspiration, theme, and form he is intensely Brazilian. He may not be Brazil's greatest novelist, but he is undoubtedly the most representative of the novelists of the Northeast.

According to an influential São Paulo critic, the early novels of Lins do Rego, particularly the five making up what he has called the Sugar-Cane Cycle, were instrumental in winning over hesitant readers to the novel of the Northeast.[13] Beginning in 1932, the novels were gathered in one a year like the yield from tropic sugar mills. *Plantation Lad* related the boyhood of Carlos de Mello. *Daffy Boy* pictured him away from home at his first school. An eddy away from the main course of the *roman fleuve* was *Black Boy Richard,* which told of Carlos' colored playmate and of his life in the city. *The Old Plantation* announced the end of the era of the senhores de engenho. Concluding the great picture of the decline of the traditional social and economic system, *The Sugar Refinery* showed at close range the true nature of the new disruptive force in society.

In the novelist's earthy treatment of a major sociological theme, Brazilian critics found what they liked to call a "telluric" quality. Particularly vivid were the books in which Carlos de Mello appeared as the central figure, incarnating more than one aspect of the author's own personality. The narrator was no pencil-and-notebook social scientist but an individual caught up in the vast social upheaval. The magnificent scope of the series caused critics to compare Lins do Rego with Hardy, Dickens, Galsworthy, Proust, and others who have presented a panoramic vision of man in society.

Lins do Rego has declared that when he began *Plantation Lad* he had in mind nothing so ambitious as a panorama of the society of the Northeast. "I wished merely to write what might be a few memoirs of a child brought up in the Big House of the Northeastern sugar plantations. I wished to relate only a segment of life. It happens, however, that a novelist is often the mere instrument of forces that lie hidden within him."[14] One work grew out of another and the author was led, so to speak, by the characters themselves to keep enlarging and adding to his first slender volume.

Plantation Lad (Menino de Engenho), the first in the cycle, contains in autobiographical form the recollected boyhood of Carlos de Mello. There is nothing that can be called a plot, merely the disconnected memories of childhood. After his demented father has killed Dona Clarisse, the boy's mother, Carlos comes to live with his grandfather, Colonel José Paulino at Santa-Rosa, where he remains until his departure to attend school. The novel describes the imprint of eight years of plantation life upon the sickly, sensitive child, who is ever threatened with inheriting his father's mental weakness and is a prey to fears and melancholy. The delicate Carlos absorbs physical strength from the earth in the tropical atmosphere of Santa-Rosa. He leads an outdoor life— swimming in the river, playing with the Negro boys, tramping the lush forests, following the workers in their task of harvesting and processing the cane into sugar loaves. These were the "good old days," near the turn of the nineteenth century and before the advent of modern industrialization to the Northeastern sugar mills.

By the time he is twelve, Carlos' initiation into the mysteries of sex is complete, for in the morally relaxed atmosphere of the bagaceira this part of a boy's education is both advanced by the tropical climate and imposed by custom. His precocious animality, however, is counteracted by a vague sense of sinfulness, and the boy is plunged into pessimism and remorse over what he considers his moral decay. "Child of perdition, child of the engenho" he calls himself as he sadly leaves for school.

In the figure of Carlos, Lins do Rego confirms some of the major sociological findings of Gilberto Freyre in *The Masters and the Slaves,* with respect not only to the material and physical aspect of society but also the less tangible psychological side of plantation life. Lins do Rego's works illustrate one of the principal themes of Freyre—that the intimacy of relations between Big House and slave quarters is a decisive factor in the formation of the Brazilian; and that the degrading influence of slavery, rather than the lasciviousness attributed to the Negro, is responsible for many vices about which, even today, many Brazilians are sensitive.

The excess of feminine caresses bestowed upon young whites, and mulattoes as well, and its opposite extreme—the freedom that was soon accorded the white boys to loaf around with the bagaceira hands, to deflower young Negro girls, to take slave women, and to abuse animals—represented vices in the upbringing of the child that were, perhaps, inseparable from the slave-holding regime under which the formation of Brazilian society took place. They are vices that explain, better than the climate and incomparably better than the doubtful effects of miscegenation upon the sexual organism of the mestizo, the precocious initiation of the Brazilian lad into the erotic life.[15]

Carlos is no mere mannequin advertising the sociological thesis of Gilberto Freyre. However, the latter's study of the formation of the Brazilian family, with special reference to the sexual patterns of the Northeastern society, does help us immeasurably to understand Carlos and the sexual theme Lins do Rego is developing.

That theme is carried further in *Daffy Boy* (*Doidinho*), the second novel of the cycle. Here, however, the novelist broadens his study to include the rough process of Carlos' education at the Institute of Our Lady of Carmo, a replica of the school Lins do Rego himself attended at Itabaiana, not far from the plantation Corredor. Now, as he leaves boyhood behind, Carlos is becoming more and more complex. We glimpse his religious development, leading to eventual skepticism; his experience with hunger and poverty; and his sympathy for the downtrodden. Carlos' animal love for the school cook is contrasted dramatically with his purer love for a schoolmate, Maria Luisa. Like the novelist himself, Carlos enjoyed reading and expressed an early penchant for writing. And always across the bright faces of the schoolboys fell the shadow of the tyrant headmaster Maciel. The man is not really a villain—his severity was simply part of the system. Lins do Rego's characterization of him is a minor masterpiece, destined to rank with that of Raul Pompéia's Aristarco in the nineteenth-century Brazilian classic *The Athenaeum (O Ateneu)*.

In *The Old Plantation (Banguê)*, Carlos de Mello is a young man in his twenties, a graduate of the School of Law at Recife. Ten years have intervened since he left Santa-Rosa, and he is profoundly changed. Showing the extent of his break with the traditions of the plantation, he says, "For me the world had grown so much that Santa-Rosa had been reduced almost to insignificance."[16] Colonel José Paulino, now a physically crumbling eighty-six, hopes his grandson will take over the direction of the plantation. The crushing disappointment of the old man's life is Carlos' inability to rise to the occasion. The indolent youth hardly stirs from his hammock in the Big House, where he spends his days reading or dreaming morbidly of himself and of his mistress in Recife.

A brief interlude with Maria Alice, the wife of a cousin of Carlos de Mello, works almost a miracle upon the nature of the young man. A new contact with life is given Carlos through the body of his paramour, and as long as she is at the plantation a spirit of warmth and cheerfulness envelops the Big House, from the kitchen, where the Negresses venerate her, to the sickroom of José Paulino, who responds for a moment to her sweet presence as a nurse. Carlos is encouraged in his sympathy for the degraded workers and is led to take seriously his position as senhor de engenho. Soon, however, the girl's husband comes for her. After she has gone Carlos is plunged into despair, from which he slowly recovers at a neighboring plantation. Later, Carlos is summoned home for the funeral of his grandfather.

The tragedy for Lins do Rego, who remembers his own grandfather, was that these men could not be replaced when they died. The doom of the patriarchal order is sounded on the screeching steam whistles of the giant sugar-cane refineries, guarantors of a new social and economic pattern. Typical of the social schism implied with the advent of large-scale enterprise is the rise of new figures to challenge the proud white barons of the past. The mulatto tenant Zé Marreira places the young planter in obligation to him, then, fawning and servile, intrigues with a near-by usina, or sugar refinery, to incorporate part of Santa-Rosa into its ever-expanding domain. The inept Carlos is saved by members of his family who band together to form their own usina. Reduced to the state of a weeping, frightened child, he sells the plantation to them and disappears.

The plantation boy is an admirably observed character, a personality with an almost infinite number of facets. We may be repelled by the figure of Carlos, particularly in *The Old Plantation,* where his spinelessness and moral fragility as an adult are not to be viewed with the indulgence accorded Carlos as a boy. The grandson of José Paulino, nevertheless, serves the novelist well in at least two respects. First, because the boy is abnormally sensitive to life and his impressions range from the noblest sentiments to the grossest and most revolting experiences, the author is able to present a complete picture of plantation life. And second, because the boy is a weakling, Lins do Rego achieves the maximum contrast between the disrupted rootless society represented by Carlos and the disappearing patriarchal traditions typified by Colonel José Paulino.

As Carlos remembered his grandfather, the old Colonel's greatest pleasure was to gaze upon his dominions, stretching out of sight in all directions: "He loved to rest his eyes upon horizons that were his. Everything he owned was destined to buy land and more land. Santa-Rosa was tiny when he had inherited it, and he had made of it a realm, extending its limits through the purchase of neighboring properties. . . . He had more than four thousand souls under his protection. A feudal lord he was, but his bondmen did not regard their servitude as an indignity."[17] From morning to night he was abroad seeing to every task of the plantation, whether the harvesting and milling of the cane, the practice of his own brand of medicine, or the meting out of justice in the manner of a medieval lord. He was outwardly severe, but those whom he called thieves and rascals knew his generosity. His conscience was serene, and his bastard offspring working in the fields caused him none of the remorse that Carlos was to feel, in *The Old Plantation,* when confronted by his own mulatto child. He feared no man, needed no bodyguards to guarantee his safety, and his enemies, as Carlos says, were "rather those of the family than his own."[18]

Carlos used to wish that his grandfather were more like the romantic senhores de engenho who protected murderers, maintained private armies, and fought for their land, instead of being a frugal and industrious farmer. Carlos thus described his grandfather in *The Old Plantation:* "Sunk in the earth like a tree, he set down roots and sent forth branches. And no one has ever heard of trees taking holidays or resting for a moment."[19] The boy considered his grandfather to have two vanities: he was proud of his caste and looked down upon the *camumbembes,* or "trash," of his family who had fallen to lower social stations; and, unaware that education away from the land alienated young men from that which they were expected to venerate, he wanted his sons to become lawyers.

The outlines of José Paulino's character may be studied in numbers of sociological and historical studies, and with special understanding in Gilberto Freyre's great work, *The Masters and the Slaves*. However, the full-length portrait of the typical senhor de engenho of the nineteenth century is that of José Paulino, as it appears in the first three novels of the Sugar-Cane Cycle. Out of affection and esteem Lins do Rego has created a towering character for Brazilian literature.

After finishing *The Old Plantation,* Lins announced his intention to proceed with *The Sugar Refinery,* logically next in the series. However, when he began to write of Ricardo, he found himself captivated by the *moleque,* whose history he then set down in a long novel.[20]

Black Boy Richard (*O Moleque Ricardo*) belongs chronologically to a time preceding that of *The Old Plantation*. It is the story of Carlos de Mello's colored playmate and of his flight from the plantation to a different sort of existence in the city of Recife, where he comes to work for Alexandre, a Portuguese baker. On his rounds as a deliveryman Ricardo meets Guiomar, his first sweetheart, and later Isaura, the yellow-skinned mulatto who appeals to his basest passions. He also becomes a friend of Pai Lucas, the *feiticeiro,* or priest, of a fetish cult, who, clinging to the African past, is at a loss to understand the younger generation of dark-skinned Brazilians and their desire to improve their economic lot. A shy and gentle youth, Ricardo is at first loath to associate with his fellow workers who want to participate in labor strikes. Later, his attitude changes, but not before he has seen much of life in the poor districts of Recife and has taken on the responsibilities of a wife who is slowly dying of consumption; and not before his own spirit, once light and carefree, has been permeated by the sadness of life around him and he has become "more of a slave than on the plantation."

The sociological aspect of the novel derives from Ricardo's continual comparison of life in the city with that on the plantation. Indirectly, Lins do Rego is substantiating, from his own experience and observation, the findings of Gilberto Freyre concerning the often benign treatment of slaves and their descendants on the great plantations of the Northeast. Under the paternalism of Colonel José Paulino the workers were better sheltered, though living in hovels, and were better cared for than their counterparts in the city, where hunger was always present. Ricardo, profoundly homesick, wishes he had remained at Santa-Rosa, even though he probably would have finished up "on the end of a hoe" in the forced labor of the field gang. After the death of his wife, Ricardo decides to join a general strike, which, ostensibly for the benefit of the working classes, is in reality only a maneuver by high-placed politicians to win personal advantage. The strike fails; Ricardo and his friends are deported to the island of Fernando de Noronha as "dangerous agitators."

Nowhere better than in *Black Boy Richard* does Lins do Rego reveal his ability to depict humanity at the lower social levels. Ricardo is presented not merely in a sketch, as are many of Lins' characters, but rather as the protagonist of an entire novel. Perhaps it is because Ricardo is much like Carlos de Mello that the author knows him so well. The characterization of Ricardo's companions, also, is done very naturally. Throughout these novels, as Olívio Montenegro has observed, Lins do Rego seems to be attracted by the physical side of man. Ricardo and his friends, who are above all creatures of instinct, are to the novelist "lyrical and sensual, innocent and brutal at the same time."[21] It is curious that an aristocrat like Lins do Rego should be one of the best Brazilian interpreters of the masses.

The fifth novel, *The Sugar Refinery* (*Usina*), deals with the inmates on the prison island of Fernando de Noronha. Lins do Rego has been censured for treating the matter of sexual perversion, but it is as a psychologist (at least not as a sensationalist) that he studies the relationship between Ricardo and Manuel, a three-time murderer from the sertão. Only in the prison atmosphere has the Negro boy been able to feel that anyone really cared for him, and when the ship comes from the mainland to take him back Ricardo does not wish to return. In the novels of the Northeast, this is not the first prisoner from the lower classes to prefer incarceration to the realities of the outside world.

After an absence of eight years, the moleque returns to Santa-Rosa to find that all has changed since the incorporation of the old plantation into the larger domain of Bom Jesús (Sweet Jesus), the sugar refinery established by old José Paulino's son Juca and other members of the family. It is significant that Santa-Rosa has lost even its name. To feed the voracious usina, new rows of cane have been planted where once the laborers and tenants lived, the old *senzala* of the Negresses has been razed, and an iron grating bars the entrance of the workers to the Big House kitchen where formerly they had always been welcome. The change from engenho to usina implies a new way of life.

As master of the sugar refinery, Juca shows much of the skill of his ancestors in cultivating the soil, and he betrays the great weakness for women which his father José Paulino had shown. A man of the modern generation, however, Juca has forgotten his obligation to the people he employs. He lacks what Lins do Rego called the "moral grandeur" of the Colonel. But some of the old man's inner goodness has been preserved in the character of Dona Dondon, Juca's wife, a woman of simple tastes and genuine affection for the plantation workers.

Although Bom Jesús prospers, its splendor is only momentary. Juca's health fails and the great enterprise is threatened. Life becomes easier for the refinery workers, who once more are able to cultivate their own plots of ground, which had recently been usurped by the cane. But their plantings are stripped by swarms of migrant sertanejos fleeing from drought in the hinterlands. Ricardo is killed when he attempts to throw open the doors of the company store, which is bulging with food the workers are too poor to buy. Finally, Juca and his family must relinquish Bom Jesús to an even larger usina. One refinery devours another, until it, in turn, is devoured by a larger; ownership is transferred to distant proprietors; the laborers are torn from their homes and set adrift. In this new pattern the usina appears as a monster of epic proportions.

Lins do Rego is perhaps the most representative of the North-eastern novelists: when writers of that region are discussed his name immediately comes to the fore. And if mention is made of the so-called novel of the Northeast, the chances are that it will be one of the novels of the Sugar-Cane Cycle. What makes Lins do Rego *the* novelist of his region? One reason is his unparalleled handling of the sociological theme: the conflict of man versus en-vironment in the changing social patterns of this land.

In characterization, a literary domain not entirely separable, in Lins do Rego's work, from the sociological, the novelist shows a special forte. He has not merely created two wonderful figures of the foreground; he has also admirably brought to life the myriad supporting figures in the five novels, who are as impor-tant, in the long run, as the principals, for it is through them that Lins do Rego is able to construct the dense social and human landscape of the novels. The intimacy existing between Big House and senzala made it possible for the novelist to know well representatives of both masters and slaves. A striking example from the Big House family is Carlos' great-aunt Sinhazinha, whose sadism is inflicted upon her Negro maids and whose evil disposition reminds Carlos of the wicked mothers-in-law of whom he has read in Portuguese legend. Another minor but still im-posing personage is the Colonel's brother, Dr. Lourenço, who keeps alive the dignity and courage of the aristocrat after the death of Carlos' grandfather. Dr. Lourenço was the only one of José Paulino's brothers who did not have a second or a third family of natural children born to Negresses of the senzala. And who could forget Tia Galdina, the old woman still enshrouded in the atmosphere of Africa, or Mãe Avelina, Ricardo's mother, and countless others of the slave hut (little transformed despite abolition)? All are done with a conviction that could have come only from a deep personal acquaintance.

And note the technique of studying these minor characters, a method depending upon the brief sketch and the carefully selected detail. His characterization of Hoarse John, the field hand, is unforgettable for all its brevity:

> Hoarse John had three children when he came to the hoe gang. His wife and children stayed home, at the clearing. More than seventy years old, he could stand up to the task as well as his youngest son. His mouth was withered and toothless, and his arms were hard and his legs strong. My grandfather's old caboclo needed no goad, and he was not subservient like the others. When Colonel José Paulino shouted at him, he would shout right back, perhaps because they were the same age and had played together as children. "Impudent rascal!"
>
> And when he needed a good man for a heavy job, out went a call for Hoarse John.[22]

With rare exceptions, the same economy is found in the description of even the major characters. We have to imagine what Carlos de Mello looked like—probably he had the family trait of "wide head and blue eyes" by which Carlos used to identify the mulatto children of José Paulino and his brothers. Details of the physical appearance of the Colonel himself—though Carlos recalls his grandfather often—are few. From scattered hints the reader gleans the impression that he is tall and solemn and wears a white beard. Is this not evidence of recalled rather than imagined personages, of whom the memory has recorded only the salient features?

Lins do Rego has remembered likewise the purely physical and material aspect of the plantation world, the feel and the look of the land, the orchards, the cotton fields, the forests; the surge of rivers depositing rich silt in the bottom lands; the growing, harvesting, and milling of the cane, on whose sticky juice a whole civilization was based. The novelist works effectively with these elements, rarely allowing them importance for themselves but rather employing them to suit his artistic purposes. He uses the land and the flora and fauna not as mere background but in the creation of mood in his characters. An example of his subjective view of nature is to be seen in the brilliant tropical settings of love scenes. The presence of Maria Alice, in *The Old Plantation,* causes the jungle to outdo itself in the production of colors and scents to make a lush canopy for the lovers. But when the girl has gone, Carlos pays little attention to the beauties of nature, and the atmosphere becomes heavy and charged with melancholy. This tone permeates literally hundreds of pages of the novels of the Sugar-Cane Cycle. Flashes of light may disturb the air of sadness—as in the gay carnival among the slum dwellers of the Mangue district in Recife—but they merely illumine by contrast the pervading gloom.

The style of Lins do Rego harmonizes well with the doleful atmosphere that is communicated through Carlos de Mello's recollections and in the novels where Ricardo appears. The language is simple and direct and, as the expression of the author's innermost feelings, intensely lyrical. The critic Alvim Correa has characterized the novelist's style as a "voice without color, nostalgic, rhythmic as the beat of waves on a beach, a monotonous sound like something that comes from afar before reaching our ear, like the wind, the sound of a bell, or a ship's horn."[23] It is a voice in which Brazilians can hear themselves speak. Not only in the relatively sparse dialogue but also in the body of the narrative, Lins do Rego has sought to remain faithful to the colloquial language, its vocabulary, its syntax, and its underlying psychology, in preference to the once consecrated literary idiom of Portugal. Perhaps for this reason the novelist has, consciously or unconsciously, allowed many traces of the regional speech of the Northeast to remain in his writing.[24]

Lins do Rego's novelistic technique marks him among his contemporaries, for it defies imitation. It is easy to identify paragraphs or even lines. His characteristic manner grows out of the memoir or soliloquy form that he used effectively in the novels of Carlos de Mello. In *Black Boy Richard* and in *The Sugar Refinery,* soliloquy is adapted to narration in the third person. The novelist describes the mental states of the chief characters, and the reader is told, or is to infer, what the character is actually in process of thinking. This device is not uncommon in literature, but Lins do Rego uses it to achieve a particular effect. Through the constant repetition of a character's thoughts, the novelist is able to reproduce the mind's obsession with an idea or attitude, as in these passages from *Black Boy Richard:*

And Ricardo stood alone in the midst of all those people who were carrying suitcases and talking at the top of their voices, who were going and coming amid festive excitement. Only now did he regret what he had done. In a swift recollection he was with his people. He remembered Avelina weeping because of him. Perhaps she thought he had drowned in the river and had placed a lighted lantern in a gourd on the waters to find him. Wherever it stopped the dead man would be located. Avelina was weeping for him. Rafael, his other brothers, were going to bed in fear for him . . . [25]

And Mãe Avelina? Why did he not go to her, to her good Negro lap? As a boy, when he suffered and was afraid, it was to his mother's lap that he ran, to the pleasant warmth of Mãe Avelina. On the plantation he would be up at dawn, milking, helping get the cattle out to pasture. Old Zé Paulino would be shouting. That kind of life was more peaceful than the oppressive one on Cravo Street. Mãe Avelina! His nostalgia for her served Ricardo as a sedative, a friendly dose to make his pangs pass away. If only he had stayed there! [26]

In this one novel there are more than twenty occasions on which Ricardo recalls his mother in similar terms. This narrative soliloquy—so called because often it is the only vehicle for advancing the main story—can be used effectively by Lins do Rego, but it becomes monotonous when it is employed hundreds of times to divulge various aspects of the Negro lad's psychology.

This technique also tends to supplant dialogue, which might well have been used in revealing character or in providing relief or variety. The scant dialogue is perhaps less noticeable in the first three novels because of the personal manner in which the story is told. In the last two novels, however, the lack of dialogue, along with the monotonous repetitions inherent in the narrative soliloquy method, cannot but weary the reader.

This is a serious defect in more than one book by José Lins do Rego. But Brazilian critics tend to minimize it. They point out that Lins do Rego is not so much a novelist as a narrator, whose style has much in common with that of the *recitadores orais,* or professional storytellers, whom he used to hear as a child in Parahyba.[27] According to Prudente de Morais Neto,

> Merely because it is not literary, in the sense given the word today, the style of Senhor Lins do Rego should not be left out of consideration; it is, on the contrary, one of the most personal, one of the most delightful, in Brazilian literature. It happens, merely, that it is not the style of writing to which we are accustomed, but rather that of the professional storyteller, imbibed directly from the fount of the living language. That is precisely what dictates the rhythm of the narrative. It might be said, even, that the action itself arises, in great part, from that source: it is the oral style which draws forth and links the episodes, which delineates the characters, which gives unity to the work, and in a certain sense accounts for its composition not as something written but as something lived. Furthermore, it is this style which permits the narrator to attain, as so often happens in his work, an almost poetic plane, an essentially lyrical interpretation of the world and its creatures.[28]

Lins do Rego writes always in haste and his novels give little evidence of polishing or retouching. Signs of inattention to detail are minor flaws and take nothing from the broad sweep of the cycle. The novelist's swift sureness makes for vigor, spontaneity and naturalness.

Other contemporary writers of the Northeast may have a better grasp of technique. Some are possibly his superiors in literary art. None, however, can challenge him as the foremost interpreter of his region. His greatest achievement has been the skillful adaptation of an individual and highly appropriate narrative form to the magnificent sociological theme that he has successfully presented with all its intensities, subtleties, and complexities.

Though differing markedly among themselves, Lins do Rego's next four novels, written in the period 1937 to 1941, have in common certain deviations from the norms of the Sugar-Cane Cycle. Why did the novelist turn aside from the family of old José Paulino? Why did he edge away from a formula that in five years had won him a major literary reputation? Obviously, to try his hand at new themes, new techniques, new locales. And, in all probability, to keep his fortunes afloat in a country where "men of talent must daily remake their intellectual reputations, by dint of new works and ever greater efforts, if they do not wish to perish completely."[29]

Whatever the explanation, Lins do Rego does set a new course, though he steers it by the charts of the earlier novels. Each of these novels has some sociological foundation, although only *Purity* has any contact with the zone of the senhores de engenho. *Wondrous Rock* and *Fresh-Water Creek* complete the novelist's tableau of the Northeast in studies of the sertão and the sandy *praias,* respectively. *The Water-Mother,* however, deals with an area remote from Lins do Rego's homeland. Since there is apparently little autobiographical basis for any of the novels, it is clear that they are imaginary in greater degree than the earlier books. In these four works Lins do Rego continues to be preoccupied with character, although there is no figure to compare with Carlos de Mello, Ricardo, or José Paulino. The simplicity and natural vigor of language, the effective creation of melancholy moods, a unique narrative style employing the memoir and the narrative soliloquy—most of the old stylistic devices remain.

This may seem to be a restatement of the successful patterns and formulas of the five previous novels, but José Lins do Rego's second phase includes only one unqualified success, *Wondrous Rock;* a rather undistinguished novel, *Purity,* which develops an insubstantial theme of sex; and two examples of the author's work at its weakest, *Fresh-Water Creek* and *The Water-Mother.*

Perhaps the last two works supply an explanation for the unevenness of the second phase: one is indebted to the Northeast only in part; the other is set in an area near Cape Frio, far to the south. The measure of Lins do Rego's success or failure appears to be the degree of his proximity to the Northeast. The novels in which he feels the firm massapé, his native earth, beneath him may be compared favorably with the best of the Sugar-Cane Cycle; those in which he wanders farthest afield suffer by comparison.

His first step is a cautious one. Timidly, perhaps even superstitiously, clinging to the plantation past, Lins do Rego produces a swiftly written work of strong affinities with the earlier novels. *Purity (Pureza)*[30] is narrated in the form of memoirs by Lourenço de Mello, who, though not a child of the engenho, is in some respects—in name even—like the Carlos of *The Old Plantation.* The scene is a tiny railroad community in the Parahyban várzea called Purity, which is surrounded by the plantations of the senhores de engenho, one of whom, a figure of slight importance for the novel, is Joca of Gamelleira, a brother of José Paulino. But *Purity* makes no pretense of being a continuation of the Sugar-Cane Cycle. The principal narrative concerns the journey of Lourenço, or Lola, as he is also called, to a house in the country, where the youth, sick in body and mind, is restored to health and manhood through a sexual attachment involving the daughters of António Cavalcanti Hollanda, a ruined aristocrat who is now the railroad stationmaster.

Readers of *The Old Plantation* will recall that in a similar manner Carlos de Mello was temporarily revivified in the luscious arms of Maria Alice. And in works subsequent to *Purity,* Lins do Rego more than once exploits the theme of the reintegration of the individual through sexual fulfillment, usually in the physical sense. Such a sexual adjustment is, in the mind of José Lins do Rego, almost always associated with the earth, with nature, and with people who live close to the land. The critic Almir de Andrade well observes that the two sisters Margarida and Maria Paula affect Lola "like air, sunlight, or the landscape of Purity."[31] The central character is emotionally unstable and, too much the creature of his sexual urge, contributes to the disintegration of the family to which the girls belong.

For Lins do Rego this is an important new theme—the decadence of aristocratic families of the region, a subject merely hinted at in earlier novels. The symbol of decline is António Cavalcanti Hollanda, the grandson of a wealthy planter, who has lost his properties through gambling and has descended so low as to condone the near-prostitution of his daughters. The theme of decadence is echoed in the conduct of Lola, who compares himself with the stationmaster and thinks that he might resemble him but for the inheritance from a rich father. The negative side of decadence is to be countered by the author in a later novel, in which out of aristocratic stagnation comes the flash of that moral grandeur Lins do Rego had admired in Colonel José Paulino.

The minor characters serve merely as background. Even the treatment of Margarida and Maria Paula is superficial, and we are at a loss to understand them as motivated by anything but sheer instinct; true, this shadowy characterization may well have been part of the novelist's design. Aside from Lola, the best figure in the novel is Lola's Negro mammy Felismena, who has reared the boy from childhood after the death of his parents. "A mother with the maternal instinct of many mothers rolled into one,"[32] her motherliness bears the imprint of slavery, and there is no indignity to which she will not stoop for Lola, even to serving him as go-between.

Stylistically, *Purity* differs little from *The Old Plantation*. Here again dialogue is replaced almost entirely by the rumina-

tions of the narrator. If the reader is fatigued by the bare simplicity of the author's style and the even tone of Lola's account,
he nevertheless gets a strong impression of the monotonous life
in the quiet hamlet. Lins do Rego has marvelously fashioned an
atmosphere to suit the brooding mental states of his protagonist.
The novel has merit as the psychological study of an aberrant
personality, but Lola's behavior is explained too much in terms
of a narrowly conceived sexuality. Focusing upon this urge,
Purity seems limited in scope in comparison with the earlier plantation novels.

Lins do Rego's first real advance in the conception of the novel
is represented by *Wondrous Rock (Pedra Bonita)*. In electing to
write a story of the sertão, he could no longer nourish the novel
on the rich recollections of his own past—memory must give
way to imagination. This new-found independence may account
for the organic strength and rightness of the book. Lins do Rego
had of course lived on the fringe of the sertão in Parahyba, had
traveled it on occasion, and had known—as what Northeasterner
had not?—many of the retirantes, or refugees, who flocked to
the seaboard in drought years. But his principal sources of knowledge of the hinterland were the itinerant poets and storytellers
whom he had heard singing the exploits of badmen, or writers
like Euclydes da Cunha, whose *Rebellion in the Backlands*
relates the historical incident at Pedra Bonita upon which *Wondrous Rock* is based.

The facts so defy belief that it is better to leave a description
of them to Euclydes himself. He tells us that the name "Wondrous Rock" was given to a pulpit-like block of stone rising among
granite cliffs in the Serra Talhada (Carved Mountains) of Pernambuco. The events taking place there in 1837 served the sociologist
as an introduction to the backlands fanaticism which he studied
in connection with the outbreak at Canudos in 1896.

A visionary mameluco or cafuso gathered together there the entire
population of the surrounding farms and, climbing upon the rock, pro-

claimed with conviction the near advent of the enchanted kingdom of Dom Sebastião. Only when the rock on which he had climbed should be broken not by the blows of a mallet but through the miraculous action of babies' blood sprinkled upon it as a holocaust, would the great king, accompanied by his shining guard, burst forth and punish inexorably an ungrateful humanity, while heaping riches upon all those who had contributed to the disenchantment.

A nervous shudder went through the sertão. The deranged man had found a suitable place for the propagation of his insane ideas. Mothers crowded around the monstrous altar holding up their tiny children and fighting with each other to make the first sacrifice. Spurting blood poured upon the rock and stood around in such quantities, according to newspapers of the time, that after the lugubrious farce had been brought to an end, it was impossible to remain in that infected spot.[33]

The fictional reënactment of this incident, all too true, in the same setting but in terms of the present day, gives direction and movement to *Wondrous Rock*.

A mutual mistrust divides the countryfolk of ranching communities around Wondrous Rock and the villagers of nearby Assu, whose ancestors, nearly a hundred years before, had slaughtered the fanatics to punish them for their superstition.

A ranch boy, António Bento, comes to Assu but is reviled by the townsfolk as a bringer of bad luck. Padre Amâncio, the saintly priest, rescues and rears him. Members of the boy's family become followers of another "saint" who appears at Wondrous Rock and claims to be a worker of miracles. On the eve of the destruction of the fanatical pilgrims by forces of twentieth-century "progress," António Bento is offered a symbolic choice between civilization and barbarism. His decision, with implications that are grave for modern Brazil, brings the climax of the novel.

Carefully studied, the town of Assu and its people are brought vividly to life. Reflecting a different sort of existence on the outlying ranges, António's mother and father, his brother who has become a bandit, and another who is a wandering minstrel and potential madman represent a social milieu in which eruptions like that at Wondrous Rock are an ever-present possibility. The characters are so numerous and varied that none, with the exception of António Bento, stands out; each seems to take his rightful place in the author's comprehensive view of the sertão.

The artistic elements of the novel are so fused in the sociological study of crime, fury, and fanaticism that we become aware of them only on deliberate second thought. *Wondrous Rock* is fabricated out of Lins do Rego's now familiar materials. There is no impression of technical innovation. The novelist has made skillful use of local legends and superstitions to ornament and extend the main theme. In *Wondrous Rock* he has conceived and executed a work broad and deep enough to rank as progeny of Euclydes da Cunha's inimitable *Rebellion in the Backlands.*

After the sertanejo of the backland and the matuto of the agricultural seaboard it was perhaps inevitable that the last panel of the Northeastern social triptych should depict the praieiro, or fisherman, who inhabits the sandy, palm-lined beaches of the coast. Unfortunately, in *Fresh-Water Creek (Riacho Doce)* the author fails to establish, as Osório de Oliveira has pointed out, that symbiosis between himself and the land and its people which he had hitherto shown in his novels of the Northeast.[34] Readers will immediately sense what is wrong: he has superimposed an extraneous and tiresome sexual drama, involving a Swedish engineer and his wife, upon his study of the peaceful and primitive society of the praieiros. Indeed, a third of the novel has its setting in Sweden, in a farm community that for all the world reminds us of a Brazilian *município* in the tropics!

This is not the first of Lins do Rego's novels to elaborate a sexual theme, but it is the first in which the subject appears to have been dragged in arbitrarily. Lola's degradation in *Purity* is legitimate in that book's social context. By contrast, in *Fresh-Water Creek* the lust-motivated plot has no real significance. Lins do Rego has sought to explain his characters, Edna, the Swedish beauty, and Nô, a robust mulatto sailor, in terms of a vague Freudianism: both were victims in childhood of tyrannical grandmothers, one a Nordic demon, the other a dark-skinned Brazilian feiticeira. But in all this, including the old feiticeira's curses upon Edna, her husband, and Nô, the novelist is sadly out of his proper element. The Swedish husband has bad luck, Nô is soon reduced to near-insanity, and Edna, likewise mentally unhinged, hurls herself into the surf, whose waters remind her of a sexual embrace. She swims away, presumably to her death, thereby completing the symbol toward which the novelist has long been visibly striving, that of the ocean-borne siren, who, in the folklore of the praieiros, lures sailors to their doom, as Edna has done, virtually, to both husband and lover.

The merit of *Fresh-Water Creek* is in the novelist's evocation of the placid life of the simple fishermen, their superstitions and folklore. Lins do Rego's effort to express in symbol an almost universal motif gives a certain dignity to the work. Another positive factor is the creation of an atmosphere of sadness and sensuality. But, although the setting is successful, the theme and characters are not. Furthermore, the technical resources commanded by Lins do Rego since his earliest novels are not improved upon. The novel is vitiated by the repetitions inherent in the storytelling device.[35]

After eight novels in as many years, Lins do Rego quite reasonably paused before publishing the strange novel *The Water-Mother (Água-Mãe)*, whose title refers to the mother liquor, or brackish sea water after the salt has been extracted. Like its predecessor, this novel attempts to be symbolic. Two of its figures, mothers of the families that appear in the novel, are, after a succession of misfortunes, reduced to something akin to the *água-mãe*.

But *The Water-Mother* is essentially a ghost story. Its irrational or superstitious elements had been paralleled earlier in *Plantation Lad*, with Carlos whistling to frighten away the werewolves; *Black Boy Richard,* in which a fetish-cult priest was a respected figure; *Wondrous Rock* and *Fresh-Water Creek,* where superstition was laced with religion. Now Lins do Rego devotes an entire novel to the story of the haunted "Blue House."

Gilberto Freyre has much to say about the Brazilian's fear of the unknown, and particularly of certain mythical creatures, generically called *bichos* (beasts), which even today strike terror in children. He considers them a heritage of the aborigine's animism and totemism.

Under Catholic forms, superficially adopted, these totemistic elements in Brazilian culture have been prolonged to this day. There are survivals easy to identify, once the varnish of European dissimulation or simulation has been scraped away. Many of them are to be found in the play and games of children in which there is an imitation of animals, either real ones or vague, imaginary, demoniac creations of the childish fancy. They are to be found also in the tales of serpents, which have a special fascination for the Brazilian young. As a sort of social memorial, inherited as it were, the Brazilian, above all in his childhood, when he is more instinctive and less intellectualized by European education, feels strangely close to the living forest, filled with animals and monsters known to him by their indigenous names and, in good part, through the experiences and superstitions of the Indians.[36]

Not only the aborigine but also the Negro, as Gilberto Freyre pointed out, has contributed to the fund of superstitious beliefs held by the Portuguese. Werneck Sodré has commented on Lins do Rego's early "education in superstition," some of which appears to remain with him to this day.[37] It is perhaps the sharing of these experiences with his Brazilian readers that accounts for the success of *The Water-Mother,* which in 1941 received the Felipe d'Oliveira Society award—a respectable prize—for the best Brazilian novel of the year.

The non-Brazilian reader might have been more impressed if the award had been for "the best Brazilian ghost story of the year." Lins do Rego is at his best in creating mysterious moods and an environment of weird sounds, wild waters, bats, screech owls, and apparitions suitable to the tale. But he has failed to give this novel any serious meaning. And we know from the symbolism of the title that he had a serious intent. The symbol may be apt, but the tragedy of the two mothers and, indeed, of all concerned lacks impact because it is the work of supernatural forces.

The locale is the salt-producing lowlands around Lake Araruama on Cape Frio in the state of Rio de Janeiro. Lins do Rego knew the area at first hand in the 'thirties, when he was engaged in the nonliterary occupation of tax collector. It is certain he never knew it intimately, however, for he evades the compelling theme of the region: the clash between the old and the new, the traditional social values of the past and those of mid-twentieth-century Brazil, as personified by opposing forces in the families concerned. He prefers to concentrate upon the Blue House and its mysteries. Dominating the novel, the house is the only real protagonist of *The Water-Mother.*

The maturation process, operating more visibly with him than with the other Northeastern novelists, can best account for the gains made by Lins do Rego in his recent works. At one level of development, an impressive story found its nearly ideal narrator; at another level, the author, casting about for fresh outlets for a remarkable talent, essayed new themes and constructed new locales with limited success. Now, with his tenth novel Lins do Rego resumes the history of the family of Colonel José Paulino, proving, as he meant to do, that "in art there are no exhausted themes, only exhausted writers."[38] His return to the Northeast, after what one critic called the "cinematographic intermezzo" of *The Water-Mother,* is an unqualified triumph. *Dead Fires (Fogo Morto)* is the masterpiece of his career.

Actually, the novelist has no more to offer in the new book than the old magic now more skillfully practiced. Stylistically, the work differs from its predecessors chiefly in a greater reliance upon dialogue—and what a difference this can make!—and in more artful handling of the familiar narrative soliloquy. Equaling if not exceeding the earlier plantation novels in the reconstruction of the social and geographic landscape of the Northeast, *Dead Fires* offers characters existing free of the morbid mind of any Carlos de Mello. In fact, the novel introduces to Brazilian fiction its first native Don Quixote, to be sure, "a miniature Don Quixote," as Álvaro Lins has called him,[30] but a creation of sufficient stature to be compared with the illustrious Spaniard.

The central theme, the decay of the proud old families of the plantation aristocracy, had already been stated in *Purity* and symbolized by António Cavalcanti. As early as *Plantation Lad* and *The Old Plantation,* Lins do Rego had sketched a plantation whose mill fires had forever been extinguished and where the "sadness of ruin, of a life's ending" hung over the *engenho de fogo morto.*

The time of *Dead Fires* is the heyday of the sugar-cane civilization in the late nineteenth century. The subject of aristocratic decadence is bound up with the history of Santa-Fe and the rise and fall of Lula de Hollanda, its epileptic master. The real-life prototype of Colonel Lula is said to have been a cousin of the novelist's maternal grandfather. Two of the other characters seem to be creatures more of fancy than of fact. The saddler José Amaro is a study in personal failure—a thistly old man whose scorn and bitterness serve to protect a tender, irritated sense of inferiority and cowardice. For the physically hideous old man, difficulties begin when an enemy circulates the rumor that he is a werewolf; in a powerful scene his wife Dona Sinhá begins to suspect that the rumor may be true. José Amaro is threatened with eviction by Colonel Lula, and at last is put in jail for refusing to leave his home.

The saddler's friend Vitorino, or Captain Vitorino Carneiro da Cunha, as he chooses to be called, comes to his defense. At first José Amaro, like everyone else in the community, looks condescendingly upon Vitorino, who, poor and unkempt as a field hand and mounted on a skinny spotted nag, is a ridiculous figure, especially when harried by a band of ragged moleques shouting obscenities at him. Even more comical, in view of the man's low social status, are his senhor de engenho airs, his grand manner of requiring deference from his "inferiors," and his habit of speaking his mind loudly on local politics. Although he is indeed a member of the aristocratic family to which Colonel José Paulino belongs, no one takes him seriously, and Vitorino is "trash."

In moral stature, however, in his unflagging devotion to justice, the old man keeps growing taller. Like Don Quixote he had his manias, but in questions of right and wrong he was reliable. In defense of the poor, the humble, the innocent, he opposes the bandit António Silvino, the militia, who are no better than the brigands, the arrogant sugar planters, including his cousin José Paulino, and the corrupt administrators of the municipality of Pilar, who are the puppets of the planters. Unlike José Paulino, whose success lies in his ability to compromise, even with the bandits who infest the region, Vitorino has a naïve dedication to his ideals that repeated beatings, insults, and incarcerations cannot shake. After he has succeeded in freeing José Amaro and others from jail through a legal maneuver, he gives vent to his characteristic defiance:

> The sharp reports of the firecrackers brought the soldiery to see what was happennig. When they saw the old fellow in the middle of the street with a burning stick in his hand, rejoicing over the victory, they approached him.
> "Stop that, you old rascal!"
> And they came toward him. Vitorino drew back against the judge's door and put his hand to his knife.
> "I'll cut down the first one who comes toward me."[40]

Both townspeople and rural planters at last come to appreciate the worth of Vitorino, in whose mind all men, big or small, have equal claim to justice. In comparison with the brooding saddler and the failing aristocrat Lula de Hollanda, old Vitorino is a staunch fortress of the noble virtues prized by the senhores de engenho. Like Lula de Hollanda, Vitorino has declined in the social echelon, but his sense of values remains patrician. Vitorino is a worthy cousin of Colonel José Paulino, who remains a very minor figure in the present novel. This is the positive side of the decadence theme, through which Lins do Rego salvages something worth treasuring out of the plantation past.

The fact that Vitorino reminds us of Cervantes' great man of La Mancha is sufficient proof of the inherent literary worth of the novel and its central character. Is it mere coincidence that the use of the road along which the characters of *Dead Fires* move corresponds to the technique of *Don Quixote?* Or that the development of the character of Vitorino from buffoonery to loftiest idealism, in the mind of the novelist, parallels the evolution of Don Quixote? It is important to record, too, his sympathy for the lowly and the old, who are the central personages of the novel. Through Vitorino, who is a mixture of the aristocrat and the plebeian, José Lins do Rego makes evident both his admiration for the moral grandeur of the planter patriarchs and his solidarity with the plain people. That he could conceive a character so richly human attests to the maturity that characterizes Lins do Rego's most creative phase.

One curious fact about the book is the absence of love, or at least of the carnal passion that often stands for it in Lins do Rego's novels. The story of Vitorino's greatness needed none of the complications of romance. Lins do Rego seems to have played down passion deliberately, preferring to express the somewhat abstract qualities of Vitorino without unnecessary emotion.

The sexual theme reappears, however, in *Eurídice*. Though its setting is Rio de Janeiro in the 1930's, the novel can be related to almost all of Lins do Rego's earlier work. Júlio, the youth who tells the story in retrospect, suggests the Carlos de Mello of the Sugar-Cane Cycle or the Lola of *Purity;* he is another of the novelist's maladjusted heroes and heroines (if we include the

warped Edna of *Fresh-Water Creek*) whose lives have been
blighted in childhood. Carlos, Lola, and Júlio have had abnormal
childhoods (as did the novelist himself), all later undergo some
kind of sexual crisis, and all relate their experiences in retrospect.
Says Júlio: "I must return to my origins, to the facts, to the
monstrous process of my formation as a man. And I cannot
escape. My memory is seized and my sensibility invaded by these
unhappy childhood days, of so much bitterness, of such cruel
wounds in my body and my spirit."[41]

The principal difference between *Eurídice* and the other autobiographical novels is that, while Carlos and Lola reveal their
psychology primarily through observation of the world around
them, Júlio subjects himself to rigorous self-analysis. He tries to
explain how he happened to commit a sexual murder. The tortured mind of the prisoner is the real theater of action. His account has the disturbing conviction of a sick man's revelations on
a psychoanalyst's couch. The imprint of Freud is particularly apparent in the early pages of the novel, where, far more successfully than in the somewhat similar study of Edna's childhood in
Fresh-Water Creek, Lins do Rego tries to account for Júlio's monstrous crime through a guilt complex arising out of a boyish
sexual attraction for his sister Isidora, who died later, as if in response to his wish that she die.

Lins do Rego creates a dense and vivid background for Júlio's
inner drama. Of the several figures at Dona Glória's pension none
are more engaging than her two daughters, Noémia and Eurídice.
The girls cannot but recall Margarida and Maria Paula Cavalcanti, the fleshly creatures who had the power of giving back the
"sap of life" to Lola of *Purity*. Strangely, there is little of physical
description of the two sisters, and nowhere are we told which is
the older, simply that both are "more or less my age."[42] Júlio says
that Eurídice is not beautiful; when he talks of her he is preoccupied with her fragrance and her body.

The girls are very different in character and temperament.

Noémia is warm and lovable, but because she reminds Júlio of his sister Isidora he is never attracted to her. Nonetheless, he remembers that Noémia, for whom he had but a comradely affection, "had called me back to life."[43]

Eurídice, quiet and inscrutable alongside her gay sister, is the novel's most brilliant characterization. In her, Lins do Rego has portrayed a human being who is pure sexual attraction. Lacking in kindness, affection, and understanding, Eurídice is another of Lins do Rego's symbolic figures: she represents the deepest and darkest of biological drives, without spiritual direction. Júlio has been warned that there is something monstrous about her; Noémia says, "Eurídice is a creature with only the form of a human being."[44] And yet Júlio felt that Eurídice had brought the first real joy to his life: she was the only woman he had ever known "who had not the slightest connection with my dead world of the past."[45] However, when she at last abandons him and when, as he says, "her words seemed to come out of the mouth of Isidora," Júlio changes from a gentle lover to a sexual murderer and strangles her.

The novel *Eurídice* has important qualities that set it apart from the other writings of Lins do Rego. Concerned primarily with an analysis of the mental aberration of the central character, it was his first psychological novel. Hitherto the novelist, although not neglecting the psychological aspects of his human figures, had, at the same time, observed the land, customs, and society of the Northeast. *Eurídice,* on the contrary, has not the least sociological interest. Even in language, Lins do Rego has flung away every vestige of the regionalism that marks the novels of the Northeast. He has thereby done no violence to his literary style, however, for the cadence and savor of his unpretentious, very popular way of writing remain. With consummate artistry, he gives an insight into an obscure corner of human consciousness, elaborating once more the universal (and at the same time very Brazilian) theme of sexual passion. In Eurídice he has created perhaps the best symbol of concupiscence to be found in Brazilian literature.

The presence of *Eurídice* among Lins do Rego's books poses a problem in regard to the over-all character of his work. From his earlier writings we might have concluded he is so much a part of the Northeast by birth and tradition that he excels artistically only when faithful to that heritage. By such reasoning, *Dead Fires,* in which Lins do Rego resumed the mighty theme of the Sugar-Cane Cycle, could be shown to crown his efforts. But *Eurídice* substantiates another point: with his most recent books Lins do Rego has reached his literary majority. *Eurídice* confirms his versatility, his ability to master, after conspicuous failures, new problems of his craft.

Although this latest novel bespeaks great possibilities for José Lins do Rego as a psychological novelist, his major importance for Brazilian literature must be said to lie in the so-called sociological novels, with their vivid reconstruction of a society and an era. Commenting on this foremost aspect of the man's work, the European critic Otto Maria Carpeaux writes:

> Conceiving of "culture" in the meaning given it by Gilberto Freyre—as the vital and human expression of life in its broadest sense, political, spiritual, social, and individual, one may say that José Lins do Rego is the literary expression of the culture of his land. . . . He is the literary conscience of the Big House and the slave hut, of the senhores de engenho and the Negroes, of the law-school "bachelors" and the moleques, of a whole world in its death throes . . . Did all this exist yesterday? Is it still as it was? Or does it exist merely in his incomparable memory? What is certain is that it will no longer be here tomorrow. It will live only in the novels of José Lins do Rego.[46]

A narrator first of all, Lins do Rego has transformed the simple, direct expression of the storytellers of his land into a vigorous and natural novelistic form. Although his writing has a regional flavor, it is in its broadest sense the language of all Brazil, a lyrical, personal language in which Lins do Rego is able to reveal the Brazilian soul.

Álvaro Lins has observed that the most noticeable of the novelist's defects remain much the same throughout his work: "They are not, however, substantial. All have to do with novelistic technique, with the art of composition, and with stylistic construction. . . . Perhaps it is more just, however, not to impose upon this novelist requirements that would perhaps tend to deform or disfigure such an original personality as his."[47] Certain defects of composition and technique arise from the author's precipitous method of writing. If his work lacks polish, he makes up for it in spontaneity and forcefulness. Monotony and repetitiousness detract somewhat, but these deficiencies are probably inherent in the novelist's narrative manner, which not only conveys graphically his Northeast but also expresses his temperament and aesthetic feelings. Like Álvaro Lins, a good many fair-minded observers seem willing to overlook certain technical flaws in view of the substantial merit of the whole of his work.

José Lins do Rego is without question aware of his novelistic shortcomings and appears to be trying to eliminate them. Particularly in *Dead Fires* and in *Eurídice* are there indications that the author, perhaps more than any other of the Northeastern writers, is capable of real growth. *Dead Fires* showed that Lins do Rego has learned to apply the psychological and philosophic wisdom acquired with maturity to the sociological theme handled effectively in the novels of the Sugar-Cane Cycle. *Eurídice* showed that Lins do Rego is no longer limited to the Northeast for themes and locales. In the eventual shift from regional emphasis to a more universal kind of writing—a tendency already visible in the nation's literature—the whole of Brazil, indeed the world itself, may legitimately become Lins do Rego's artistic domain.

CHAPTER III

JORGE AMADO

Jorge Amado

THE MOST widely known of the nordestino writers is undoubtedly Jorge Amado from Bahia. His reputation projects far abroad, and his novels have been translated into twenty-four different languages, including French, Russian, English, German, Swedish, Danish, Yiddish, and Spanish. In Europe Amado once caught the critical eye of André Gide, who commented on his work.

The European as well as the Brazilian vogue of Amado has often been the result of political rather than literary qualities. He reacted violently to his times, and some of his books have been marred by extreme partisanship to the left. Nevertheless, he is a novelist, and an important one. Brazilian literature would be deprived of several impressive works should critics decide to rule out his writings as political.

Amado was born on August 10, 1912, on a cacao plantation not far from Ilhéus in southern Bahia. His father, João Amado de Faria, had migrated from Sergipe around the turn of the century and had started to carve cacao *roças,* or plantations, out of the tropical forest. This was ever the "violent land," and Jorge early learned about the growing of the golden fruit. These and later years spent on his father's land are reflected in his "cacao cycle" of novels.

83

When João Amado de Faria's economic situation improved, he sent his twelve-year-old son to a secondary school, the Jesuit Colégio António Vieira in the city of Bahia. After a successful year, during which the lad was thought to have a vocation for the religious life, a drastic change occurred. The model student turned rebel and fled the school. After a short interval on his father's estate, he was returned to Bahia—this time, however, to the famous Ginásio Ipiranga, a school whose very purpose was to serve as a catch-all for expelled students and where "were gathered together the cream of the rebellious and insubordinate of Bahia."[1]

When he was sixteen, and while continuing his education, the novelist-to-be worked briefly as a cub reporter for a city newspaper, wrote for various literary reviews, and soon allied himself with a little group of fledgling writers, Alves Ribeiro, Dias da Costa, Clovis Amorim, Edison Carneiro, João Cordeiro, and others, who were headed by Pinheiro Viegas, an older man well known to the city's intellectuals. "You could be sure to find them in the afternoon at the Bar Bahia, discussing, over an innocent demitasse, the most recent ideas coming from Europe and São Paulo."[2] The allusion to São Paulo proves that the group was interested in the modernist movement of the late 'twenties. It was probably the modernists' demolition of the older literary standards which attracted Pinheiro Viegas and his boys, including Jorge Amado. Calling themselves the "Academy of the Rebels," they issued two short-lived publications, *Week* (*A Semana*) and *Meridian* (*Meridiana*). Werneck Sodré has it that the academy's main activity was "hurling insults."[3]

When the group was dissolved in 1930, Amado was sent by his father to Rio de Janeiro to study law. There, at the age of eighteen, he began his first novel, *Carnival Land* (*O País do Carnaval*),[4] which was published in 1932. Although devoid of literary merit, the book is worth noticing, first, for its reflection of the confusion and excitement before and after the revolution of 1930, with its boiling ideological currents, and second, for the evidence it bears of Jorge's own search as a young Brazilian for something in which to believe.

Amado's subsequent evolution in political thinking seems to have paralleled that of José Lopes, the Communist figure of *Carnival Land.* Although he did not identify himself with the Communist party until many years later, his entire career as a man of letters was intimately connected with radical political movements in Brazil during the 'thirties and thereafter. In 1946 he was elected a Communist deputy to the Brazilian congress; when the party was suppressed in May, 1947, he went into exile in Europe, from which he has recently returned for a short visit. The scion of a now wealthy family, whose fortune is said to derive from cacao, Amado continues to be the rebel of his Bahia days, uncompromising in his devotion to an extremist ideology.

With the exception of *Carnival Land,* the least typical of his works, everything that Jorge Amado has written has a sociological foundation. Brazilians themselves do not deny the fundamental truth of the situations and institutions studied by Amado. They do not tax him with misrepresentation. He is merely one of many Brazilian novelists of the 'thirties who had cause to interpret the terrible social drama of his times. Amado draws critical fire only when, unlike Lins do Rego, Graciliano Ramos, or Rachel de Queiroz, he combines the objectivity of the *document* with the impassioned subjectivity of the *protest.* Sociologists may confirm the factual portions of his writing, but must make reservations in regard to the novelist's analysis of the facts.

The question of the rightness or wrongness of Amado's sociopolitical views, or of his humanitarian philosophy, is not at issue here. From the strictly literary standpoint, however, it must be observed that such a philosophy, when projected in the novels, has grave consequences for art. Their frankly political aim requires some justification in literary works.

Studying land and people broadly, Amado has adopted the naturalistic technique of Émile Zola, whom he much admires. Like Zola, Amado admits "gathering material" for his novels.

In order to write these novels of mine (which may have every defect but which have this quality: the absolute honesty of the author) I have gone in search of the people, I have gone to live with them, since my childhood on the cacao plantations, my youth in the cafés of the capital, my trips throughout the entire state. I have cut across it by the most diverse means of travel, and I have heard and seen the loveliest and strangest of all Brazilian humanity.[5]

Amado has been charged with writing mere *reportage* and with concentrating upon the sordid and repugnant aspects of life. He is nearly always saved, however, by his temperament and novelistic skills from being just one more in a long line of Latin American Zolas.

In a short but penetrating study of the novels of Jorge Amado, the Brazilian critic Álvaro Lins divides his work into two parts, the first containing *Carnival Land, Cacao,* and *Sweat,* which are perhaps too harshly described as having an adolescent, "even a certain infantile character,"[6] and the second part embracing the remainder of his novels. The division is appropriate, for character, plot, and literary form are consistently neglected in the first phase. In fact, there is reason to believe that Amado purposely slighted artistic qualities in attempting to draft social documents. The second phase is initiated by *Jubiabá,* which reflects the author's new concern for literary technique and refinement of style.

Another division of Amado's novels might be based upon the three distinct geographical regions with which they deal: the cacao fields to the south, the city of Bahia, and the outlying sertão. Without his Northeast, Amado would, we suspect, be no novelist at all.

Carnival Land is the story of Paulo Rigger, the European-educated son of a Brazilian cacao grower, and of his search for a philosophy of life. Morally adrift, Rigger seeks happiness first in the cultivation of his instincts, particularly the sexual. Later he has a love affair with a girl of the lower classes, abandoning her when his social prejudices assert themselves. He becomes a journalist and a follower of an old intellectual of Bahia, Pedro Ticiano, who gathers about him a small band of younger men dissatisfied with their generation and anxious for new solutions to their problems. Religion, politics, love, marriage, and philosophy are discussed, usually in a bar, with the noisy vehemence of youth turning over new ideas. Probably the most revealing state-ment of the novel is this: "Truth is a very relative thing. There must be a particular truth for each man. That which brings serenity is for him the supreme truth." To which Paulo Rigger replies, in all seriousness, "Incredible!"[7]

Amado himself acknowledges the artificiality of these char-acters, who are puppets acting out, or merely mouthing, their respective philosophies. Ricardo Braz attempts to find happiness in love and marriage. Gomes, the venal manager of a newspaper founded by the group, seeks wealth in local politics. Jerónimo Soares joins the Catholic Church, and José Lopes, the best-in-formed and most articulate of the group, emerges with a brief for man, material values, and communism. The declared intention of the novelist is to discredit the skepticism and pessimism of old Ticiano, the mentor whose influence is flung off by all his youth-ful admirers. Rigger finds no belief to suit him and departs once more from his "carnival land."

The author is to be linked with the fictitious Paulo Rigger, for he says in the preface to *Carnival Land:* "I fight for no special cause. I am still one of the searchers." And also: "This book is an outcry, almost a plea for help. It is an entire dissatisfied genera-tion in search of its goal. We now begin our fight against doubt. The new generation combats skeptical attitudes."[8] This novel, in which Amado cannot be accused of partisanship, although he does express dissatisfaction with things as they exist, shows the novelist in a rare moment of indecision.

The rather primitive work is full of the impulsiveness and impatience to be expected of a youth of eighteen. With "magnificent audacity," as a critic observes,[9] Amado attempted the novel of ideas, a genre which, because of his lack of culture and maturity, he must reduce to his own plane of art and understanding.

Amado has written three novels about cacao. Their scene is southern Bahia, which since the middle of the nineteenth century has been the center of Brazil's richest area of production of the so-called "chocolate bean." *Cacao (Cacáu)*,[10] his first attempt at portraying the region, was a rather crude sketch of life on a plantation near Ilhéus. From all parts of the Northeast, migrant workers come each year to harvest the multicolored pods, which, hanging from trunks and branches, have been compared to Chinese lanterns casting a beautiful but unreal glow on the jungle. Amado describes the culture of a modern "forbidden fruit"—because of its economic value, denied to the undernourished workers by the growers—and he details the appallingly low standard of living among the *alugados,* mostly Negroes, mulattoes, and poor whites, who "rent themselves" to the contractors for the harvest and are often slaves to their unpaid bills at the planter's commissary.

The prostitutes in the cacao region, old at twenty, are victims of the harsh Brazilian sexual code about which the novel's slender plot revolves. When the planter's son seduces the sweetheart of a workman, Colodino, the latter stabs him, and is aided in his escape by the Negro jagunço hired to kill him—an example of "class consciousness"—and becomes a leftist organizer. One of the motives for social protest is the fact that the seducer is not even censured, while his victim is forced into prostitution. Sociologists acknowledge the existence of this Brazilian practice. As literature, however, this immature novel founders because of its idealogical bias.

The *Sergipano* (man from Sergipe) is the real hero of *Cacao.* Though a worker, he has the opportunity to marry the planter's daughter, but chooses instead to better his class. "I looked without longing at the Big House. Love for my class, for the workers of the city and country, a great human love would slay my sterile love for the boss's daughter. That is how I thought," concludes the Sergipano, "and I was right."[11]

In strong contrast is the next novel of the cacao cycle, which appeared ten years later. Of all his works, *The Violent Land (Terras do Sem Fim)*[12] remains Amado's masterpiece, a story of almost epic grandeur. This description of the struggle between rival planters for possession of the cacao groves is the only novel by Amado that contains no propaganda. Is it because the time of the action, at the turn of the century, was unsuitable for a story with political undertones? A better explanation is that the novelist had a sincere admiration for the *fazendeiros*. These were heroic men he had known himself: his own father was a cacao planter, "one of those Sergipanos who as a child came to Bahia to build a country, who crossed sertões, opened roads, raised cities," in forty years of effort in Bahia, "through the force of his heroism and the poetry of his life."[13]

The contenders in this "violent land" were veritable armies of fazendeiros, their workers, and hired assassins (jagunços); their prize was a strip of unexploited forest.

The forest lay sleeping its uninterrupted sleep. Over it passed the days and the nights. The summer sun shone upon it. The winter rains fell upon it. The tree trunks were hundreds of years old, an eternal greenness sweeping down from the hills, invading the plain, becoming lost in the infinite. It was like an unexplored sea, locked in its own mystery. It was like a virgin whose body had never known the call of desire. And like a virgin it was lovely, radiant, and young, despite its centenary trees. Mysterious as the flesh of a woman not as yet possessed, it too was now greatly desired.[14]

The fundamental theme that links the several novels of cacao —the eventual enslavement of all to the cacao pod—is beautifully stated in *The Violent Land.*

The workers in the cacao groves had the cacao slime on their feet. It became a thick crust that no water could ever wash off. And all of them, workers, jagunços, colonels, lawyers, doctors, merchants, and exporters, all had the cacao slime sticking to their souls, inside them, deep down in their hearts. Education, culture, decency—these were powerless to wash it away. Cacao was money, power, everything in life. Not only was it planted in the black, sap-giving earth: it was also inside themselves. It arose within every one of them, casting its dark shadow over every heart, crushing all good impulses.[15]

Fighting for the golden fruit were the Badarós—Juca, his brother Sinhô, and the latter's daughter Don'Ana—and Colonel Horácio Silveira. Although the Badarós are aristocratic and Colonel Horácio is plebeian, they are alike in their passion for the land, their veneration of brute force, and their quest for power. Cacao has leveled them. Individual differences, however, sharpen the characterizations. Sinhô Badaró hates killing but kills nonetheless, especially when he can find a passage from the family Bible to justify him. Horácio's great weaknesses are cacao and his young wife Ester.

Slender and pale, of a beauty tinged with sadness, she was the only thing that could make Colonel Horácio smile in a way different from his usual one. But at this moment he was not thinking of Ester; he was not thinking of anything. He saw only the tiny fruit of the cacao trees, as yet still green, the first to be produced by that grove. With his hand he touched one of them; gently and voluptuously he caressed it. Gently and voluptuously as if he were caressing Ester's young flesh. Lovingly. With an infinite love.[16]

Ester, however, repays his crude veneration by an affair with the Colonel's lawyer Virgílio. After Ester's death and Horácio's discovery of her letters to Virgílio, his decision to put the lawyer "out of the way" comes as naturally as his next breath.

The war between Horácio and the Badarós brings out the heroic qualities of Don'Ana Badaró, a fearless girl who is as ready as her Uncle Juca to kill in defense of the estate. She has a manly quality, despite the tawny beauty and the dark eyes that inspire

João Magalhães to marry her, after he has first promised old Sinhô to adopt the Badaró name. Struck by her bravery, Colonel Horácio forbears killing Don'Ana after his victorious siege of the Badaró Big House, which inflicts ruin upon the fortune of his enemies.

Artistically the best of his novels, *The Violent Land* shows what Amado can achieve when art is not encumbered with the millstone of political argument. The hostility and proletarian purpose which in *Cacao* made of the fazendeiro a fat, mean-eyed ogre exploiting his workers are absent from the characterizations of Juca and Sinhô Badaró and Colonel Horácio Silveira, who are among the novelist's most acute psychological studies.

Both the Colonel and Don'Ana, as well as the latter's husband, João Magalhães, reappear in *St. George of Ilhéus (São Jorge dos Ilhéus)*, which describes the cacao economy in terms of the present day. The central action is the seizure of the land from the fazendeiros by a group of exporters who employ a different means of conquest. There is some historical basis for this: during the First World War the planters mortgaged their rapidly expanding estates, which were later lost to the banks in the postwar economic collapse. Since then there have been few resident owners, few arrogant colonels.[17]

To suit Jorge Amado's special propagandistic purposes, however, the historical time of the novel is moved to the 'thirties, when the exporters, cornering much of the South American cacao market, plot to raise the price of the product in order to cause expansion and inflation. When the planters have become overextended, the exporters will cut the price of cacao in the world market, the planters will default on their loans, and the exporters, holding mortgages, will then foreclose and take over the plantations. Such is the "capitalist plot," as seen by Amado.

Fortunately for the novel as literature, he has infused life and movement into his study of Ilhéus, "Queen of the Southland," in successive periods of "boom and bust." The complicated plot, involving exporters, planters, workers, labor agitators, Communists,

Integralistas, and, for added spice, assorted cabaret entertainers, is skillfully handled. Amado repeats from the preceding work a number of effective scenes dealing with cacao cultivation, political intrigue, and the technique of the notorious *caxixe,* or "ouster," by means of which owners are dispossessed of their property, as through the recording of forged documents in the legal registers.

Old Colonel Horácio Silveira, vanquisher of the Badarós, is adept at the caxixe maneuver, and as long as he lives remains the lord of the region. Don'Ana, though impoverished by him, cannot but admire his defiance of the exporters. When he has a political opponent put out of the way, she is obliged to say, "There is a man!" As in the preceding novel, these and other lesser fazendeiros, such as Maneca Dantas, Teodoro das Baraúnas, and António Víctor and his wife Raimunda, are remarkably consistent. We rely on their verisimilitude all the more when we realize that Amado, in order to create these exploiters, is going against the ideological grain.

In his novels dealing with the historic city of São Salvador da Bahia de Todos os Santos, or Bahia, Amado exhibits many of the qualities found in the cacao cycle. There are moments of supreme artistry but, probably more often, moments when art is absent. The early work *Sweat* is on a par with the proletarian *Cacao;* likewise a bit sketchy and vindictive, it is also crudely realistic. *Jubiabá* reveals the hand of one who could create *The Violent Land;* sometimes argued to be Amado's best, *Jubiabá* at least deserves to rank alongside that book. Two other novels of the cycle display the good and bad characteristics of Amado, the excessive attachment to the proletarian theme set over against a first-rate storytelling talent that makes his work readable.

In almost all these novels Amado has been able to capture the mystery that he says flows like oil upon the city. He has caught the spirit of "the mother of all Brazilian cities." Historically the first Brazilian metropolis, Bahia is also called "black Rome," because, even though it is a place of imposing Catholic churches and basilicas, one many also hear African drums booming from the Negro districts, where the fetish cults, or *candomblés,* are still very much in existence. In no Brazilian city is the influence of Africa more evident. It is truly "a medieval city surrounded by African villages."[18]

Bahia may also be viewed in terms of the rich and the poor rather than in terms of black and white. Indeed, although the juxtaposition of Negro and European is a valid one, there are to be found in Bahia, as in all Brazil, whites, blacks, mulattoes, and other mix bloods in all the economic categories. Social distances are measured in degrees of economic class rather than in terms of race or caste, as, for example, in the United States. Donald Pierson in his study of the Negro in Bahia has said, "The struggle for position in Brazil, therefore, takes on some of the character of a class-struggle in the Marxian sense."[19]

Amado is the novelist of this class struggle in the lowest social echelon. *Sweat (Suor)*[20] describes one of the proletarian quarters of Bahia. Like Michael Gold's *Jews without Money,* which is widely known in Latin America and has influenced Amado, *Sweat* is rather a propagandist's notebook than a novel in the usual sense. It is a sheaf of sketches of types observed at 68 Whipping Post Hill, a vast tenement where Amado lived in 1928 and which he describes in his more recent guidebook to the city:

Formerly the nobility lived here. These multi-storied town houses, their tile façades now replaced by blue or purple paint, sheltered distinguished families. Opposite them was the whipping post. Negro slaves came to be disciplined; from the balconies the young ladies gaily watched the spectacle. Blood from the Negroes' backs flowed upon the stones, their cries filled the air. The great old mansions of Whipping Post Hill are still full of those piercing shrieks, the hill is full of sorrow and suffering which is prolonged even today among the modern slaves of the tenements.[21]

Since there are no central characters, unity is supplied by the tenement itself; the account is given a political orientation when its inhabitants join in a mass protest against the arrest of strikers and are fired upon by police. Bitter in tone, the novel's depressing view of life is almost unrelieved. Despite the author's ability to record incident vividly and to capture the essence of lower-class speech, *Sweat,* more than any of the novelist's other books, deserves to be called reporting. No one, however, could deny the truthfulness and power of the book as a record of man's brutality to man.

Jubiabá,[22] Amado's fourth book, and second in the series on Bahia, marks an important advance in his conception of the novel. Hitherto he had been feeling his way, first with *Carnival Land,* then with the two short novels *Cacao* and *Sweat,* both strongly in the proletarian vein and purposely (it would seem) without literary adornment. Originally Amado may have felt it a political obligation to keep his novels as lean and unprepossessing as the people he described. The change came in 1935, when, after reading certain opinions expressed about the novel by participants in a writers' congress in Paris that year, Amado became aware of the need to be more painstaking in the technique and organization of his work.[23] He then wrote *Jubiabá,* which is surely a minor masterpiece of the literature of the 'thirties. The proletarian theme remains, but thereafter he stated it more artistically, often symbolically.

The late Artur Ramos, Brazil's eminent anthropologist and student of the Negro, has called *Jubiabá* "a novel permeated with the odor of Bahia; a novel of the religion and rites of the Bahia Negroes and a work in which the Negro tells his own fascinating story."[24] It should be considered a product of the campaign during the 'thirties in Brazil to vindicate the Negro, who, always wearing the badge of slavery, ascends more slowly in the social scale than any other part of the population. Everywhere Amado champions the black man, and nowhere more effectively than in his Negro hero António Balduíno.

Born in a quarter of Bahia in which the African footprint is still visible, Balduíno is a moleque of the streets who "was pure as an animal and knew only the law of the instincts."[25] The lad is consumed with hatred for his oppressors. After a boyhood spent between the Negro district and the fine home of a Portuguese who momentarily befriends him, the lad becomes the leader of a band of homeless waifs, and, eventually, a *malandro,* or good-for-nothing, who strums his guitar, composes sambas, drinks rum, learns the art of *capoeira* fighting, and pays passionate court to the *mulatas* of the city.

Balduíno's unrequited love for Lindinalva, the white daughter of his benefactor, may be regarded as a symbol of the Negro's unconscious quest for purity. Lindinalva did not even know of Balduíno's lifelong devotion. When she dies a prostitute, he maintains that she was chaste and that only he had been her husband. "When I went out with a woman I always had her in my mind."[26]

After successes and one great failure as a boxing champion, and various adventures while wandering through the outlying agricultural districts, Balduíno, still the malandro, returns to Bahia. There, for the first time in his life, he becomes a working man, then a labor agitator, and in this pursuit finds a new purpose and usefulness in life. His sudden conversion from aimless malandro to a man of social awareness belongs in the realm of the miraculous, but because he is a myth it is easier to accept this social miracle.

Amado's technique in the creation of Balduíno has been called distortion by Gilberto Freyre, who compares his technique in this respect with that of the painter El Greco. "Such distortions are to be found in some of the pages of Jorge Amado, for instance, where purely visional truth is freely exceeded by the poetic and sometimes political dramatizations of situations."[27] The novelist may have sought to represent a typical Negro of the present; if so, he has failed, for the result is a figure cloaked in poetry and presented far larger than life. To appreciate the degree of distortion, compare José Lins do Rego's far different treatment of a modern Brazilian Negro, the gentle, homesick boy Ricardo, who haltingly adjusts himself to his new situation in Recife. Artur Ramos has commented on this difference of approach: Lins do Rego's Sugar-Cane Cycle contains "more serene considerations and reflections, in which the Negro is analyzed as an element in a civilization in which the sugar economy predominates"; Jorge Amado, on the other hand, is "interested in race vindication . . ."[28]

As a Negro of the present, Balduíno stands in striking contrast to the Negro Jubiabá, from whom the novel takes its name and around whom the African cultural survivals in Bahia are studied. Unlike the heroic Balduíno, Jubiabá is sketched from real life, according to Amado. The hundred-year-old man is a *pai de santo,* or leader of a fetish cult, at whose *terreiro,* or temple, the religious ceremonies called candomblé, or *macumba,* are observed. Amado was himself an *ogan,* or male initiate, of a Bahian fetish cult, and his undisputed knowledge of Negro life is based on personal experience.

A high point of the novel is the author's description of a candomblé, in which the female ceremonial dancers (*filhas de santo*) whirl about Jubiabá and his retinue of ogans until "made" (*feitas*), or possessed, by the spirit of one of the African deities (*orixás*).

All in the room danced as if mad to the sound of the drums, the cymbals, the rattles, the gourds. And the orixás danced too to the sound of the old African music. In the person of the feitas four of them were dancing around the ogans. Then, writhing on the floor were Oxossí, god of the hunt, Xangô, god of lightning and thunder, Omolú, god of smallpox, and Oxalá, the greatest of them all.[29]

Through his charms and *despachos,* or offerings, to the ancient deities, Jubiabá also served as witch doctor (feiticeiro) to Balduíno and others, curing their illnesses, giving them supernatural strength, and avenging their enemies.

Like Pai Lucas of *Black Boy Richard,* Jubiabá symbolizes the African past, which, as assimilation progresses, is fast disappearing. In a final scene, illustrating the new symbolism in Amado's novels of political outcry, Jubiabá bows to the Negro Balduíno after the latter has participated in a successful general strike against the city. "And Jubiabá, the witch doctor, bent before him as if he were Oxolufã, old Oxalá, the greatest of all saints."[30]

The novelist of the Negro, Amado may also be called the Brazilian novelist of the sea, which is an indispensable part of the Brazilian scene. With him, the sea becomes another personage of the novel. In *Sea of the Dead (Mar Morto)*[31] Amado describes the maritime life of the city, and especially of the men who sail the small, sturdy sailing vessels, known as *saveiros,* that ply between Bahia and the little ports of the Recôncavo or along the Paraguassu River. One of Amado's most lyrical novels, *Sea of the Dead* is a web of adventure and of superstition. The chief characters are Guma, a mulatto sailor, and his sweetheart Lívia, who fears the sea goddess Yemanjá. Here the action of the novel is poetically foreshadowed:

> Yemanjá punishes. She never shows herself to men except when they die at sea. Those who die in storms are her favorites. And those who die to save others, those go with her, like the ships, visiting all ports, sailing all seas. No one ever finds their bodies, for they have gone with Yemanjá. To see the mother of waters many have flung themselves smiling into the sea, never to appear again. Can she be asleep with all of them in the depths?[32]

Yemanjá is another of the African deities frequently met in the Bahian novels of Amado. Even to this day fishermen and their families make yearly offerings to the *mãe d'água* (mother of waters), whose fetish is the sea shell and who may be called Janayna, Inaê, the Princess of Aioká, or simply Maria.[33]

With the folklore elements Amado has artistically integrated his message of social protest: after Guma drowns during a heroic rescue at sea, his wife, though a landlubber, goes to sea in her husband's saveiro, thus "fighting back," as Amado calls it, against her destiny, against the grinding poverty that condemns the seamen to a bare subsistence.

Around the saveiro sea birds wheel and pass close to Lívia's head. She stands erect, and thinking that on the next voyage she will bring her son, whose destiny is the sea. Maria Clara's voice is suddenly hushed, because, as dawn breaks, a Negro is singing, taming the mysterious sea: *Hail morning star.*

Morning star. On the pier old Francisco is shaking his head. Once before, when he did what no other sailboat skipper would ever do, he had seen Yemanjá, mistress of the sea. And is that not she whom he now sees, standing on the *Flying Packet?* Is that not she? It is she, all right. It is Yemanjá who is sailing there. Old Francisco shouts to the others on the wharf:

"Look! Look! It's Janayna."

They looked and they saw. Dona Dulce watched too from her schoolroom window. She saw a strong woman who was fighting back. This fighting back was her miracle. It was beginning to come about. On the wharf the sailors could see Yemanjá of the five names. Old Francisco kept shouting—it was the second time he had seen her.[34]

Amado's sentimental conception of the primitively "pure" lower classes may be carried too far, as in his final novel of Bahia, *The Beach Waifs (Capitães da Areia)*.[35] A band of homeless urchins, "dressed in tatters, filthy, half starved, aggressive, hurling obscenities and smoking cigarette butts, were, in truth, the lords of the city: they knew it completely, they loved it completely, they were its poets."[36] Some forty of them live in an abandoned warehouse near the beach, boys with nicknames like "Peter Bullet," "Big John," "Professor," "Limpy," "Skinny," "The Cat"— each a symbol of a racial or social type. The group has innumerable adventures, brawls, beatings, thefts, imprisonments, escapes, and sex experiences. "Lords of the city" these children may have been to Amado—they were nonetheless a social menace, which the novelist shrugs off with sentimental pleadings.

They stole, fought in the streets, called people names, caught little Negro girls on the beach, and at times they wounded men or the police with their razors or knives. Still, they were good, they were friends to each other. If they did all that, it was because they had no home, or father, or mother; their life was one of not eating regularly and of sleeping in a big building with hardly any roof. If they had not done that, they would have died of hunger, because the houses were rare where food was given to one or clothing to another. And not even the entire city could give enough for all of them.[37]

When the gang breaks up, the boys drift into various pursuits, several to become criminals, one a friar, another a "bum," and one a famous painter. Sem Pernas ("Limpy"), his brain afire with hatred for all mankind, flings himself off a precipice rather than be captured by police. Pedro Bala, whose father had been killed in a strike years before, becomes leader of a shock brigade, and later a revolutionary, Comrade Peter Bullet, "who was pursued by the police of five states as the organizer of strikes, as the director of illegal parties, as a dangerous enemy of the established order."[38]

The novel is replete with pathetic scenes demanding an emotional response: Pirulito's theft of a statue of the Christ-child, Pedro Bala's punishments in a reformatory, Boa Vida's self-sacrifice in quarantining himself in a compound from which few return alive, and the death scene of Dora, who was "mother, sister, and sweetheart" to the gang of urchins. The critic is never sure whether Amado's sentimentality is not merely an immoderate expression of the author's compassion for the unhappy humanity he describes. One thing, however, is certain: lack of restraint is a defect in his novels.

Another deficiency seems to be magnified in *The Beach Waifs.* The death of Dora would have been no less tragic without the detail of her sudden reaching of puberty that made possible her marriage to Pedro Bala. The question of poor taste resulting from Amado's preoccupation with sexual mores, especially deviations from normality, may well be considered in the light of the fact that the novelist seeks to tell the truth about his characters, especially those of the lower classes, whose obscene language and crude behavior he describes with the utmost realism. The charge of pornography sometimes leveled at Amado would seem to depend upon the man's intention in presenting questionable scenes, and in view of his sincerity it would seem just to point out a lack of artistic sense rather than to accuse him of sensationalism. *Palavrões* (obscenities) in the work of Amado have often been commented upon, but nowhere better summed up than by Andrade Muricy, who speaks of Amado's "literary heroism equivalent to that of Cambronne on the field of battle."[39]

The Beach Waifs was a product of its times. Some episodes are effectively described, and possess literary value. In general, however, the book's angry spirit and obvious propaganda for a political party negate most of its worth. In 1937, the year of its appearance, it was, along with the earlier and equally contentious *Cacao,* banned in Brazil. All the novelist's works have been banned in Portugal.[40]

Jorge Amado's most recent novel, *Red Harvest (Seara Vermelha*), has as its setting the same forbidding Bahian backlands described by Euclydes da Cunha. Like José Lins do Rego, Amado concerns himself with fanaticism and banditry, but his penchant for social problems as texts for political preachment causes him to study a further problem associated with the sertão: the migration of sertanejo families, uprooted by the loss of their lands or by drought, who journey more than a thousand miles, by way of the São Francisco River, to the "promised land" of São Paulo.

Amado blames the latifundiary system of landholding for the plight of the old mulatto farmer Jerónimo, who, after being forced off the land he had worked for years as a sharecropper, sets out with a little band of children, grandchildren, and others— thirteen in number, including a goat and a cat—to seek work in the south. In a journey which would make that of the Joads of *The Grapes of Wrath* appear a pleasure outing in comparison, Jerónimo's group disintegrates, either through starvation in the *caatinga,* disease aboard an overcrowded river vessel, or other misfortunes—such as the daughter's resorting to prostitution in order to get a bill of health for her tuberculous old father, who straightway ostracizes her.

In the sertão, says the novelist, "hunger creates bandits and saints,"[41] and in the novel the themes of banditry and fanaticism are tightly joined. The climax is the bloody destruction of the pilgrim followers of "Blessed Stephen," along with the bandit forces who revere him, by government soldiers. Calling the episode "a new Canudos," Amado admittedly relies upon Euclydes' earlier study, but, with his usual flair for the novelesque, symbolizes the fratricidal aspect of these backland wars by opposing as enemies two of the sons of Jerónimo, the soldier João and the *cangaceiro* Zé Trovoada, who escapes into the wilderness of thorny bush which is the caatinga.

The epigraph of the present novel announces that "in the latifundiary system, in the poor distribution of territorial property, in the monopoly of land, lies the fundamental cause of the backwardness, the misery, and the ignorance of our people," a statement by Luis Carlos Prestes. But Sérgio Milliet, a competent sociologist as well as literary critic, noting that this is a main point in Brazilian Communist doctrine, points out that subsidiary causes offer a more valid explanation for fanaticism and banditry, for example, the lack of education, of justice, of economic opportunity, and of religious training in the forsaken sertões of Brazil.[42]

The merits of *Red Harvest,* which are to be found in vivid scenes and action-filled episodes, are virtually nullified by a final chapter (comprising one-fifth of the novel) dealing with the Communist-abetted revolution of 1935 by the National Liberation Alliance. The link with the preceding portions of the novel is the character Juvêncio (or Nenén), another of Jerónimo's sons, who runs away from home and becomes a Communist conspirator. The final episode is jarringly inappropriate, suggesting that in this latest work, if not in the majority of the earlier novels, Amado has used his talents to disseminate a political message.

In plot construction, characterization, and other phases of novelistic technique, the author's *parti pris* leads him to commit errors. In his effort to prove the thesis that the masses are unjustly exploited and should unite against their oppressors, Amado gives to his novels a broad sameness that permits the reader to predict with accuracy the final outcome of nearly any plot situation. Aside from *Carnival Land* and *The Violent Land,* both of which are unrepresentative (one because of its weakness, the other because of its strength), the story pattern of the novels is generally that of *Cacao,* in which the workers, after long enduring their economic servitude, are driven to collective action in a strike or some act of violence.

Sweat, Jubiabá, Sea of the Dead, and *The Beach Waifs* follow the same plot formula as *Cacao,* although after *Sweat* the stories contain more complication and are more subtle. The exhortation to arise and fight against oppression may be given a more artistic and symbolic form, as in *Sea of the Dead,* in which the urge to class struggle is made part of a folklore motif. Of the later novels, written in the 'forties, both *St. George of Ilhéus* and *Red Harvest* run true to type, except that, curiously, in the former it is not so much the lower classes as the fazendeiros themselves who are exploited and dispossessed by "capitalists." One cacao planter actually joins a leftist movement; some capitulate to their new masters; others, notably the Sergipano António Víctor and his wife Raimunda, workers who had become landowners, die defending their roças.

In the foreword, Amado, who has never been one to proceed by stealth, advertises his Marxian interpretation of the historical facts (altered, of course, to suit his purpose) upon which *St. George of Ilhéus* is based. "And if the drama of the feudal conquest is epic and that of the imperialist conquest is merely ordinary, it is not the fault of the novelist. Joaquim [a Communist character] says that the coming stage will be filled with heroism, beauty, and poetry, and this I believe."[43] These remarks may also be the novelist's justification for having written so warmly of the fazendeiro class in *The Violent Land,* an ideological failing he attempts to remedy in *St. George of Ilhéus.* Here, though it is based on a "rudimentary Marxism," as one critic noted, Amado's writing is distinctly Communist, and not simply radical, in tone. The Communist Joaquim, a militant proletarian, like Nenén of *Red Harvest* exemplifies Communist teachings.[44] In the earlier novels, although communism is sometimes discussed,[45] working-class heroes—Isaac of *Sweat,* various unnamed agitators of *Jubiabá,* and João Adão of *The Beach Waifs*—are allied with unspecified union movements rather than with "the Party," as in the two later novels. In the last-mentioned work, the most violent in a revolutionary sense, Pedro Bala, though a militant proletarian and revolutionist, is not linked specifically with communism.

Such characters are frequently mere stereotypes, political notions turned into men. The degree to which Amado's ideological bias warps his view of humanity is well illustrated by the fact that he is inclined to place his characters in one of two categories: good or bad. Among the latter are the fazendeiros, their overseers, the regular clergy (particularly the higher officials), and, sweepingly, the rich, the police, and the soldiery. Another evildoer is "the American," who may be a strikebreaker or a well-to-do businessman. In *Sweat,* a motion picture produced in the United States and critical of the Russian Revolution of 1917 is accused of misrepresentation.[46]

Into the realm of the good go the agitators, the militant proletarians, all strikers, the workers, the poor, the upper-class sympathizers, and, it would appear, all criminals, for they are "determined" by an unjust social and economic order. Besides murderers and thieves, there is a multitude of sexual perverts. Apology is made for all these, unless they betray their friends or class, as did the lubricious Esmeralda of *Sea of the Dead,* whom the author drowns. The famed bandit of the Northeast, Virgulino

Ferreira Lampião, who was killed by the police of Alagoas in 1938, is introduced as an epic figure in *The Beach Waifs*.

> Only the caatinga belongs to everyone, because Lampião set the caatinga free, expelled the rich from the caatinga, made the caatinga a land of bandits who fight against the fazendeiros. The hero Lampião, hero of the whole sertão for five states around. They say he is a criminal, a heartless cangaceiro, a killer, a rapist, a thief. But for Volta Seca, for the men, women, and children of the sertão, he is a new Zumbí dos Palmares [a Negro hero of the seventeenth century], he is a liberator, a captain of a new army. Because liberty is like the sun, the world's greatest possession. And Lampião fights, kills, deflowers, and steals for freedom, for freedom and justice for the exploited men of the immense sertão . . ."[47]

Such effusions can be turned on and off at will. When Amado later wrote the history of the Prestes Column and learned that Lampião, then fighting for the government, had opposed Prestes, he treated his erstwhile hero contemptuously as one who "deflowered virgins, killed the innocent, castrated men, robbed the rich and the poor alike."[48]

The continual intervention of the author's political animus, the frequent homilies on class solidarity and the need for action,[49] the fact that most of the novels end in a strike, all count against the novelist. What is surprising is that he succeeds in holding the reader's interest.

Not all the characters are to be placed alongside Lampião, the militant proletarians, the "good" labor agitators, the "bad" foreign businessmen. Some of them, despite being two-dimensional and relatively uncomplicated, are so strikingly achieved that they are almost unforgettable! Rosenda Rosedá, the "velvety mulatto" ballerina of the pathetic little backlands circus of *Jubiabá;* Francisco, the old sea-worn sailor of *Sea of the Dead,* reduced to mending nets on the beach; Pirulito, the urchin of *The Beach Waifs* who seeks God in the gutters of Bahia; and the doctor of *Red Harvest,* who is driven to alcoholism by the eyes of tuberculous sertanejos seeking an impossible bill of health in order to continue their journey to find refuge in São Paulo. As Olívio Montenegro says of them,

Whether the figures of Jorge Amado's novels are authentic or not, they impress us through the moving force of their action, through their animal exuberance and, at the same time, through their innocence of spirit, their simple and human impulses. They are probably authentic, up to a certain point of observation, and thereafter, imaginary. And the more imaginary the better.[50]

The saving feature in all the novels of the second group is the novelist's imagination, his "guardian angel," as Montenegro once observed. "Unlike some other realist authors, Jorge Amado has an imagination that does not become sterile in contact with reality, is not diminished and sucked dry by facts; rather, these are re-absorbed by the imagination, which brings them to life with a new, more dramatic force and impregnates them with mystery."[51] Realism is the point of departure for Amado's art, but, after the novel *Sweat,* there is a new note of lyricism, if lyricism is taken to be a synthesis of the author's feelings toward life expressed in terms of symbol, figurative language, and rhythmic prose.

In a typical instance of reality transformed, or, if one prefers, "distorted" for artistic purposes, the Negro António Balduíno, after being beaten in a prize fight, hears the African drums of the macumba pounding in the night, like the pulse of blood in his temples, and is reminded of all the centuries of the black man's servitude.

Eram sons de batuque que desciam de todos os morros, sons que do outro lado do mar haviam sido sons guerreiros, batuques que ressoavam para anunciar combates e caçadas. Hoje eram sons de súplica, vozes escravas pedindo socorro, legiões de negros de mãos estendidas para os céus. Alguns daquêles prêtos que já tinham a carapinha branca, guardavam nas costas marcas de chicote. Hoje as macumbas e os candomblés enviavam aquêles sons perdidos.[52]

In the Portuguese we can appreciate the measured drumming of the author's prose, which here makes use of the onomatopoetic value of the word *sons,* several times repeated, and of the evocative power of the African terms *batuque, macumba,* and *candomblé.*

Other poetic qualities, particularly Amado's emotional intensity and his use of figurative language, are well illustrated in the description of a storm which opens the novel *Sea of the Dead:*

Night had come ahead of time. No one was expecting it when it fell in heavy clouds upon the city. The wharf lights were as yet not lit. In the Lighthouse of the Stars there were as yet no tiny lamps lighting up the rum glasses. Many saveiros were still crossing the waters of the sea when the wind brought the black-clouded night.

Men looked questioningly at each other. They looked out upon the blue of the ocean to ask the origin of that night which came before its time. It was not yet time. Meanwhile, preceded by the cold crepuscular wind and laden with clouds, it came on, deadening the sunlight as if by some terrible miracle.

Night arrived without its usual musical greeting. The bright voice of the bells at eventide had not echoed through the city. As yet no Negro had appeared, guitar in hand, upon the sandy beach. No accordion was welcoming night from the bow of a sailboat. Not even the monotonous drumbeat of the candomblés and macumbas had rolled down along the slopes. Why then had night closed in without waiting for the music, without waiting for the sign from the bells, the rhythms of the guitars and accordions, the mysterious beat of the ritual drums? Why had it thus come inopportunely, ahead of time?[53]

Characteristic of Amado is the simplicity of this poetry-in-prose. The lack of complexity, in vocabulary as in imagery, points to the fact that the author is writing for the widest possible segment of the Brazilian reading public.

Now and then Amado tries to re-create the essence of balladry as he introduces the poetic *ABC* into his narrative or imitates its lilting rhythm.[54] Sérgio Milliet points out that a long prose passage in *The Violent Land* goes naturally into lines of seven syllables:

Era uma vez três irmãs:
Maria, Lúcia, Violeta,
unidas nas correrias,
unidas nas gargalhadas.
Lúcia, a das negras tranças;
Violeta, a dos olhos mortos;
Maria, a mais moça das três.
Era uma vez três irmãs,
Unidas no seu destino.[55]

The ballad rhythm is usually not so obvious as in the passage quoted, but the simple phrasing and the tone of his language are often those of the folk poet or *cantador* regaling his listeners with a tale of adventure and heroism.

In comparison with Lins do Rego, Amado makes far more effective use of dialogue, which is usually realistic, and serves as a counterbalance for the many lyrical descriptions and narrations. Through dialogue the reader is always returned to the flesh-and-bone world of reality.

Amado employs the vernacular in all his writing. He goes out of his way to avoid anything that might be called "literature," in the pejorative meaning the word sometimes had among writers of his generation. His sentences have little or no stylistic grace and appear to be set down, often in haste, in a monotonous fashion. However, although he is no architect of the sentence, Amado can impart to his language "a savor as of flesh, and a rhythm almost like music," as Olívio Montenegro has observed.[56] This critic also makes an appropriate comparison of the language of Amado with that of José Lins do Rego. Both know the simple, artless speech of the people, and both are indebted to the popular poets and storytellers of the Northeast.

Amado's stories have something strangely in common with the epic poems of the Middle Ages, in their disregard for proportion, their admiration for the hero, the preference for action over character, and, finally, a wonderful mingling of the fancied and the real. He has always depended on episodes, not always well integrated, to give movement to the novel. In reviewing his total work, we think not of precisely constructed plots but rather of a succession of episodes, some of which, taken individually, are nothing short of masterpieces.

In the works of this most controversial of modern Brazilian writers, unevenness is the salient characteristic. Amado seems to write solely by instinct. Of conscious art intellectually arrived at, the result of reflection and high craftsmanship, there is relatively little. Yet his novels have a mysterious power to sweep the reader along. Serious defects in artistry are overcome by the novelist's ability to weave a story, to construct vivid scenes, and to create fascinating characters. "An incomplete and mutilated novelist," as Álvaro Lins has well characterized him, he offers the "spectacle of a great talent for creating fiction in contrast with enormous deficiencies as a writer and as an intellectual."[57] Though his literary career now covers more than twenty years, Jorge Amado is barely forty years old. No writer holds out a greater promise, and his future works will be eagerly read by those who expect the promise, made manifest in *The Violent Land,* some day to be fulfilled.

CHAPTER IV

GRACILIANO RAMOS

Graciliano Ramos

THE RECENT DEATH of Graciliano Ramos makes it possible to view as a whole the work of one who may be considered Brazil's greatest novelist since Machado de Assis. Like Machado at the end of the Second Empire, Ramos was something of an enigma to his contemporaries, and already he is half hidden in legend. Fifty years hence, biographers and critics may still be seeking the real Graciliano. Though many have written fragments about him, there is no complete account of his life. Recently an invaluable document has appeared, written by Ramos himself—a loosely linked collection of autobiographical sketches entitled *Childhood (Infância)*. This last major work before his death contains clues to his personality as well as to the novels.

Possessed of a literary culture greater than that of any of the novelists of the generation of 1930, Ramos had far less formal education.[1] Reared and formed remote from civilization in the sertão, he has often been described as a "cultured sertanejo." He was born in the interior of Alagoas, at Quebrângulo, on October 27, 1892. As an infant he was taken with his family to the ranch of his grandparents in the sertão of Pernambuco, near Buíque. When the boy was about five, a severe drought, the periodic seca, caused the financial ruin of his father, a small merchant of Portuguese extraction who had tried to become a cattle rancher. The family then moved to tiny Buíque, where the father set up a store. When Graciliano was seven the family moved back to the state of Alagoas, to the municipality of Viçosa, where the boy's primary schooling was to continue until he was twelve.

Thanks to his autobiography, these eleven formative years stand out with amazing clarity. They are important because their imprint is strong upon two of the novels, *Parched Lives* and *Anguish*. (It is curious that Ramos' last two novels turned back to his earliest recollections for their themes and setting.) Through *Childhood* we learn that it was in the sertão, in an atmosphere of dazzling sands and rock, of vast open spaces of dead vegetation, that the boy first knew real thirst under the broiling sun. Here he learned the life of the cowherd, inspected the stone fences, the corrals, and the goat pens, and first saw the luminous sky crossed by flights of black birds departing the parched land. No wonder the novelist knew so well how the sertanejo Fabiano of *Parched Lives* lived and thought and felt.

Many of the characters who people the novel *Anguish* were acquaintances of the author: the rancher who was the boy's grandfather, the *cabra* José Bahia, the old Negress Quitéria, as well as the minor figures of the washerwoman Rosenda, Father Inácio, and the police corporal José da Luz. Early experiences, recounted in *Childhood,* were incorporated into the novels; a true incident is the rancher's payment of tribute to the backlands bandits, the cangaceiros, who later, as an act of courtesy, hide in the underbrush in order not to frighten his wife when she comes along the road.[2]

We glimpse the probable origin of Ramos' misanthropy in the restrained account, free from sentimentality or self-pity, of his bleak childhood, of a stern and authoritarian father and an irascible mother who reared him with cuffs and blows. The autobiography is full of unflattering judgments of his father Sebastião, who, because of his connection with important families of the sugar-cane

aristocracy around Viçosa, was appointed judge of the municipality. In the eyes of his son, however, the judge did not incarnate
fairness, and his dispensation of justice frequently miscarried,
whether with respect to the boy himself or to others.

Once, when the beggar "Flat-Nose" came into the Ramos
house, the judge was so upset by his presence that he had him
arrested and jailed. Graciliano's commentary:

> I felt disgust, repugnance, a vague remorse. I had not ventured a
> word of compassion. I would have gained nothing; my intervention
> would surely have been prejudicial, but I ought to have faced the con-
> sequences of it. I had witnessed an injustice, and I considered myself an
> accomplice. Cowardice.
>
> Later, when they ceased punishing me, I became insolent and gruff at
> home—and I believe that Flat-Nose's imprisonment thus had its in-
> fluence. It must also have contributed to the distrust which I have for
> authority.[3]

In the novels of Graciliano, justice—especially social justice—
seems always to have miscarried.

Other details from *Childhood* acquaint us with the awkward,
unkempt, physically ugly boy, who had a tendency to nervous
ailments. Learning to read, to the accompaniment of the ferrule,
was a physical as well as a mental process. His boyhood curiosity
about stories, his "affection for lies," as he termed it, developed
into a mania for reading. Before he was twelve he was digesting,
in translation to be sure, Zola, Hugo, and Gorki, along with such
nationals as Alencar and Aluízio de Azevedo. Money to buy
books was stolen from Sebastião Ramos' store till: "These crimes
caused me no remorse. I was able to convince myself that my
father, distant and stingy by nature, tacitly approved them."[4]
Even at that time Graciliano hoped to become a novelist and had
already begun to write stories for a literary review that flourished
briefly in Viçosa—attempts, some have thought, to find refuge
from the hated world of reality.

At the age of twelve he was sent to the capital city of Maceió to receive secondary schooling; of this period there are a few recollections in *Anguish*. However, he left the course uncompleted. This marked the end of his formal education—a happy event, thinks Werneck Sodré, for it allowed Graciliano the chance to educate himself outside the "official wisdom" of such schools.[5] Returning to Viçosa, the boy entered upon a period of intensified mental activity which included the reading of Dostoevski, Balzac, and Eça de Queiroz. All of these, particularly Eça, had an influence upon his later writings.

The recollections of Viçosa, which has been described as "the Brazilian municipality with the highest rate of crime—one and a half murders per day,"[6] are important as a basis for another of Ramos' novels, *St. Bernard* (*São Bernardo*), which is set in the same fertile agricultural belt of the littoral that Lins do Rego studied. Some of the violent episodes in the novel had been observed at first hand, as we learn in a passage from *Childhood*.

Old man Frade, influential in a neighboring municipality, used to say that he had never killed a man. He had killed mean cabras, plenty of mean cabras. In my municipality men also were assassinated, although mean cabras were preferred. When a landholder friendly with the government wanted to annoy an adversary, he had someone eliminate some of the man's workers—and the threatened person sold him the land for less than its value. If he did not sell right away, more "help" kept disappearing, until the transaction was completed. Only rarely, in cases of personal affront, family issues, were members of the upper class eliminated. Property was taken from these by more or less legal means. But the rabble was decimated, old man Frade's mean cabras died in abundance, and people got used to cadavers spotting the city.[7]

The fictional Paulo Honório of *St. Bernard* is a product of such a background. Graciliano has called him a "composite of certain hard-hearted landowners of the Northeast," but he has also said that his own father's "stern face [*carranca*] and bits of old narrations by him were combined in the building of Paulo Honório."[8]

About 1910 Graciliano's father moved his family once more

to the sertão grazing and cotton-growing community of Palmeira dos Índios, in Alagoas, where Graciliano was to stay, with one noteworthy absence, until 1930. The absence occurred when Graciliano, a virtual outcast from the family because of his literary aspirations, went as a young man of twenty-one to Rio de Janeiro to become a newspaperman. Although there are few details about these and succeeding years, we do know that the venture in the capital failed and that he returned to Palmeira dos Índios in 1915, presumably to the dreary provincial life he has pictured in *Caetés,* with its setting in the sertão community.

There, like his father, he became a merchant, but he never forgot his earlier interest in literature. In the late 1920's he was elected mayor of Palmeira dos Índios, where as owner of a general store—"stock market, forum, agora, cenacle, library, and casino for the town'"—he was held in respect as one of the wisest of men. José Lins do Rego, later to become a friend of Graciliano, has described his first uneasy encounter with "the man who knew the most mythology in all the sertão.'"[10] And this "quiet sertanejo with the unfriendly face, distrustful eyes, and bitter smile," as Lins do Rego recalls him, really did know his mythology, and along with it the English, French, and Italian languages and literatures, not to mention a great deal about human nature, as he was to demonstrate in his novels.

As mayor of Palmeira dos Índios, Ramos gained prominence when one of his reports to the state government concerning social and economic problems in his prefecture—a report drafted with precise command of language—provoked widespread controversy in the national press, and he was invited to contribute articles to newspapers. The famed publisher and poet Augusto Frederico Schmidt asked him to submit a novel. *Caetés,* which Ramos had had on hand since 1926, was sent to Rio de Janeiro, where it was enthusiastically received. In 1933, the year of its publication, the author was already in his forties. His second novel, *St. Bernard,* gained an even greater success in the following year.

Ramos was thus an established writer with a national reputation when a tragic series of events, unquestionably related to the revolutionary ferment of the middle 'thirties, brought him great personal suffering. In the early 'thirties he had gone to Maceió to become director of the state school system, in which he tried against tremendous odds to institute reforms. At the end of 1935, after the uprising of the National Liberation Alliance forces, he was shipped to Rio de Janeiro and held prisoner on a penal isle, to the great detriment of his health. Some say that his was a purely political arrest; others allude to "mysterious small-town intrigues,"[11] which may refer to enmities resulting from his attempted reforms in Maceió. Whatever the reason for his incarceration, this period was one of torment for the novelist. Readers of the third novel, *Anguish* (1936), should connect the tortured narrative of Luis Silva with these dark days in Ramos' own life. In his declining years he lived obscurely, supporting himself in the long-familiar atmosphere of newsprint and linotypes as a proofreader (he insisted he wrote nothing himself) for a large Rio de Janeiro daily.[12]

One writer mentions Ramos' "political idealism which has caused him so much injury,"[13] a reference to his well-known radical leanings. However, although there is much implicit social criticism, nothing in Ramos' work would serve directly as political propaganda. Presumably, he was dedicated to some sort of reorganization of society. Yet he seems to imply in his writings that attempts at improvement are futile and that happiness for man is an impossibility. The social reformers, the humanitarians, come to naught in their efforts: one of them is forced to commit suicide; others are made to appear ridiculous. In the opinion of several discerning critics, it is extremely difficult to reconcile the distinctly unhumanitarian philosophy of Ramos with his radical political beliefs.[14]

Floriano Gonçalves, a well-informed critic of the novelist, finds the key to Ramos' social thinking in the "terrible determinism" that rules the lives of his characters. The novelist's pessimism, he believes, is not extended to all men but solely to the individual of the society and economic situation of the Northeast. The nordestino is condemned to suffer as long as the bases of society remain as they are. Says Gonçalves: "Only a change in the framework of forces which surround him and crush him will be able to transform the Caeté, the brute, José Bahia, and Fabiano. In this respect the art of Graciliano Ramos is the most intensely revolutionary of any of living Brazilian writers. His thoughts have a logical end, and revolution is an essential necessity within the social setting which he paints."[115] This "logical end" of the novelist's thinking must be supplied by the speculative critic. However, Gonçalves' interpretation deals squarely with the attitude of Ramos toward society and is probably the most convincing. He takes into account the author's constant preoccupation with the nature of society and its pressures acting upon his characters. From this obvious fact as well as from Ramos' known political radicalism, Gonçalves draws his conclusion that the novelist is a revolutionary writer. Yet such works as *Anguish* and *St. Bernard* are in no sense propaganda—their meaning is too cryptic to have doctrinary value. Furthermore, Ramos is too innately a literary artist to create a novel for any political end.

An entirely different interpretation of Ramos' inner meaning is that of the European critic Otto Maria Carpeaux, who holds that the novelist's attitude toward social change is one of irony. Carpeaux says that Ramos is aware of the ridiculousness of attempting to change the social structure through revolution.

I am sufficiently well acquainted with his convictions to be convinced, for my own part, that they represent merely the surface of his thought. They are not transformable into art; and this is significant. Luis Padilha and the Jew Moisés [a minor figure of *Anguish*] are not revolutionary heroes. Every time the novelist gives in to the temptation to formulate programs of social reform—the schoolteacher Magdalena talks in these terms—he falls right into the trap of his most detested enemy: the commonplace; in this case, the humanitarian commonplace concerning "generosity" . . .[16]

"Merely the surface of his thought," then, is Ramos' personal political belief, and his work is far from having a revolutionary meaning. Carpeaux offers an ingenious interpretation of the novels in relation to the personality of their creator: they are seen as subconscious attempts to destroy the agonizing world of the author's memories, the city, civilization,—the pitfalls of his characters—in order to return to the relatively tranquil world of the sertão from which he, like his characters, has come.[17]

Although provocative, Carpeaux's thesis leaves out of account the sociological groundwork on which all the novels, after *Caetés,* rest. Ramos' comparison of the relative purity of sertanejo society with the corrupt environment of the littoral, a fundamental social theme, is not subconsciously introduced, but is a basic idea. Simply because the theme is given an unprecedented artistic form, so that it is always on a secondary plane, we cannot dismiss Ramos as a social thinker. This is not to detract from his work as a psychological novelist, but to affirm his significance as a sociological novelist as well.

The personality of the novelist constitutes another puzzle. The phrase "cultured sertanejo" seems to sum up best his contradictions and conflicts. As a literary man, Ramos had to make his mark in the comparatively brilliant and refined society of the coastal cities, but, despite the critical acclaim given him as one of the foremost writers of Brazil, he appeared unable to accept the civilization of the capital. To those who knew him best, he remained the unvarnished sertanejo, or country "hick." A pose? Modesty? In all likelihood neither. Through his resistance to the comforts and adornments of civilization, through his sharp criticism of the men and institutions of the littoral, he probably was expressing the vaunted individualism of the dweller of the backlands, particularly of the sertanejo frustrated in his desire to return to the sertão. Always at odds with the civilization to which he owed his renown, he seems to have been a tragic misfit in society.

As Álvaro Lins has said, "The question of whether or not one accepts the entire conception of life which arises out of the novels of Graciliano Ramos should not prevent anyone from admiring the artist who upholds it."[18] Ramos has come to grips with the major theme of his time, that of social man against the land. To give it intensity and clarity, he has presented it in the minds of individual men. And to make it permanently endure, he has cast the whole—four short novels—into the time-resistant shape of great art.

According to Osório Borba, a shrewd Brazilian observer, we must go to the novels themselves in search of Graciliano Ramos.

I know of no work [*St. Bernard*] that better portrays its author, not that it is completely and rigorously autobiographical. But in the person of the author one cannot help seeing the physical appearance of Paulo Honório, a demoralized and brutalized senhor de engenho, his fifty years spent in useless endeavor, and persisting in perpetuating the memory of a stupid and sterile existence because of a literary whim late in life. People often call Graciliano "Fabiano." Paulo Honório, Fabiano, Luis Silva, Seu Tomás, Padilha, a gallery of restless failures, victims of one knows not what inner maladjustments, of a conflict between ambition and weakness, concocting evil thoughts, in a constant fermentation of dissatisfaction toward life, muttering obscenities against humanity and against themselves. . . . In each of these figures, a bit of self-portraiture.[19]

Only a novel like *Dom Casmurro* of Machado de Assis could stand comparison with the modern-day achievements of Graciliano Ramos in the realm of the psychological novel. Like Machado, Ramos was an acute student of character who saw life with irony and pessimism. He is distinguished from his predecessor by his insistence upon the social theme, and from his fellow nordestinos by his greater interest in character. In the last quarter of a century, he has been the outstanding psychological novelist of Brazil, and his tormented protagonists are frequently compared with Dostoevski's creations. In the depressing, inwardly seething mental world he portrays, his heroes carry heavy mental burdens, and their terrible thoughts are systematically explored.

The soul's "highest aspirations to love, to sincerity, to beauty, to piety, struggle violently in the clutches of barbarous instinct, of animal cruelty, of the eternal denial of beliefs and sentiments that are seemingly the most sincere."[20] To Ramos men are simply animals, complicated animals, to be sure, who are subject only to the conditioning of their physical and social environment, who fight to survive in hostile surroundings, and who are wretched creatures deprived of the possibility of happiness. Rats, dogs, pigs, beasts—these are often the symbols for man in the pages of his novels.

Ramos' first novel is the least inclined toward psychological exploration. In *Caetés,* however, the characters fit into the author's pessimistic scheme of things. In this novel he showed that man's notions of right and wrong, indeed of all ethical values, are determined by nothing but self-interest.

The novel's ironic title *Caetés,* which relates to the question of the relativity of moral values, comes from the name of a cannibalistic Indian tribe inhabiting the Northeast at the time of the conquest. João Valério, as the story opens, is writing a novel about them, but advances no farther than the second chapter, for, as he says, "I have no way of knowing what goes on in the mind of a cannibal."[21] In the course of Ramos' often wryly humorous novel, the reader begins to perceive, along with João Valério, that the youth has much in common with the cannibal Caetés: "What am I if not a savage, lightly polished, with a tenuous coat of varnish on the outside? Four hundred years of civilization, different races, different customs. And I said I did not know what happened in the mind of a Caeté! Probably what happens in my own, with a few differences."[22]

The setting is Palmeira dos Índios, a quiet, dusty backlands town where life is monotonous. João Valério falls in love with the wife of his employer and benefactor, Adrião Teixeira. No sooner does the affair reach the adulterous stage than Adrião is informed of it. João Valério manages to convince his friend of his "innocence," whereupon Adrião remorsefully commits suicide for having doubted his wife's fidelity. Later, the lovers discover that their love has withered.

João Valério's seduction of the wife of a friend, his denial of the affair to Adrião, his callous acceptance of the man's deathbed apology, and his solicitude in seeing that the suicide is buried with appropriate lamentations, all run counter to established social ethics. Valério's behavior is motivated by immediate self-interest. And nowhere does he show remorse. "The recollection of Adrião's death little by little vanished from my mind. After all, I need not trouble myself over something which I could not help. My guilt is not great, for there are numerous men who have been bothered by unfaithful wives. I am unable to suffer for long."[23] Adrião's wife Luisa, despite the admirable moral qualities attributed to her by João Valério, despite her conjugal dignity and her generous sentiments for the poor, is at length seen to be a "Caeté" herself, "a sensitive creature who, needing to love someone, had preferred me to Dr. Liberato or Pinheiro, the young men who frequented her house."[24] João Valério's conclusion concerning his relationship with Luisa is simply that he has discovered "a law of nature." As Ramos sees it, all human activity and especially all ethical, religious, and social values are subordinate to this "law."

The underlying materialistic philosophy of *Caetés* links it with the rest of the novels. However, though published in 1933, it had lain in a drawer since 1926. This time factor in a period of literary evolution is important for *Caetés* and explains why it is so different from the rest of Ramos' works. *Caetés* is a novel in the nineteenth-century tradition of a Flaubert or an Eça de Queiroz. There is no sustained interest in the sociological, and the language still retains a certain refinement that was to be discarded when the novelists of the early 'thirties embraced the vernacular. In its structure *Caetés* points to an earlier day than the 'thirties, when it actually appeared. The critic Floriano Gonçalves assigns to

Eça de Queiroz the major influence shaping the novel: "In his initial work it was Eça de Queiroz who gave it the structure of the French novel, with well-balanced chapters, much movement, and a great deal of dialogue. From Eça, above all, comes his taste for delineating his figures in caricature."[25] Gonçalves points out the absence of monologues (despite the book's being related in the first person) that were to make possible the introspection of *St. Bernard* and *Anguish*.

Although Ramos' first novel is his least impressive accomplishment, it does succeed in reconstructing the oppressive and tedious atmosphere of a Northeastern small town, where men and women of superficial culture and civilization are provoked to act like the primitive Indians who occupied the land before them. A remarkable feature is the treatment of minor characters, who, in their movement and sharp delineation, recall the villagers of *Madame Bovary*. Furthermore, *Caetés* is commendably broad in its scope. Ramos' study of the bases of social ethics is applied to an insignificant person of the Brazilian Northeast, but his conclusions have applications everywhere. There is little attempt to invoke the regional or sociological background in order to explain João Valério. In the mid-twenties, when the book was conceived, character evidently did not have the fascination it was to have for Ramos in the early 'thirties, when the sociological novel appeared.

In *Caetés* his preoccupation with the nature of the novel is shown, exaggerated, of course, in the character of João Valério. Satirically the novelist conveys his aversion for the so-called regional novel, with its obscure vocabulary of native terms ("My aim was in reality to employ a tremendously effective word: *tibicoara*"),[26] its picturesque figures (various Caeté types), and its melodramatic action (the cooking of the human victim, the recipe for which João Valério, substituting goat for human flesh, obtains from his landlady).

For Ramos the novel must deal with human life here and now.

Regional and sociological elements must be integrated with the characters themselves. A passage from *Caetés* exemplifies the manner in which a description of nature is used to delineate character.

Mountains to the left, near, green; mountains to the right, distant, blue; mountains in the background, very distant, white, almost invisible, in the direction of the São Francisco River. I lit a cigarette. And dejectedly I mused that there was in me something of that landscape: a vast plain surrounded by mountains. . . . Hopes and fears that devour me are easily exhausted in brief journeys in this flat and bare expanse which is my life.[27]

In *St. Bernard (São Bernardo)* the Brazilian novel attains its most dignified and artistic form. Although presented in miniature, the elements making up the society of the cane-growing littoral of Alagoas are as carefully handled as in the best of José Lins do Rego's sociological novels. The ways of agricultural life, the cotton fields, the ginning, the cattle grazing, are integral parts of the story. And the human types are familiar to anyone who knows the Northeast: the cabras, the sertanejo overseer, the declining rural aristocracy, and Ramos' specialties—the small-town newspaper editor, the parish priest, the lawyer, and the politician, urban types well set off against the rural. More important, the sociological theme remains secondary. The reader is aware of it only as background and is likely to consider *St. Bernard* primarily a psychological novel.

In this second novel by Ramos, the method used is the first-person narrative of a man who reviews his past actions in a state of mental turmoil. Paulo Honório, conditioned by his physical, social, and psychological environment, has risen from obscure parentage. As a boy he led a blind beggar and was later "mothered" by a Negress candy-seller, old Margarida. He is driven by relentless ambition to become the master of the fazenda St. Bernard, where he once did the brutalizing work of a hired hand. Paulo Honório's is a success story based upon shameless

methods of advancement, from petty cheating and political op-
portunism to murder. This heartless backlands *arriviste* marries
a young schoolteacher; the result is a violent conflict between man
and wife as well as within the man himself. The presence of
young Padilha, the penniless but educated *doutor* whom Paulo
has bilked out of his ancestral estate, provides a powerful irritant
to Paulo's egoism: jealousy. Life on the plantation is made unbearable for Magdalena, who, although innocent of infidelity,
poisons herself. Her husband afterward learns that part of a letter
from Magdalena he had found and assumed to be destined for
another was in reality his wife's suicide note to him.

Paulo is telling his story as a distraction, after Magdalena's
death. He feels old, and life has no meaning for him. "How many
useless hours! For a person to consume his entire life without
knowing for what reasons! Eating and sleeping like a pig. Like
a pig! Getting up early every morning to run out and look for
food! And then stocking food for one's children, for one's grandchildren, for many generations. What stupidity! How revolting!
Would it not be better for the devil to come and take all?"[28] Men
are animals. Some, like his friends the priest and the lawyer, are
domesticated; others, like Casimiro Lopes, the sertanejo overseer,
are in the wild state. And Paulo Honório, despite his ability to
read and his interest in writing these memoirs, places himself
in a category little if any higher. Happiness for him is an impossibility; he does, however, muse: "If I had kept on scouring
old Margarida's copper pan, she and I would have had a quiet
existence. We would have spoken little, thought little, and at
night, after coffee and sugar, we would have prayed, on the mat,
our African prayers, in the grace of God."[29] The memory of
Magdalena torments him, reminding him of the ruin of his own
life as well as hers. But, "if it were possible to start all over again,
exactly the same thing would happen. I cannot change myself,
and that is what disturbs me."[30]

Graciliano Ramos' hard-hearted philosophy of man is recapitu-

lated in the words "brutality" and "egoism" as Paulo Honório
applies them to himself. His is the law of the herd, of every man
for himself, of the survival of the fittest. Thus oriented, Paulo
remains in a state of shock when confronted by those who have
more civilized ideals. Thus he comes to view Magdalena, with
her ideas of social betterment, as a Communist who poses a threat
to himself. Although the thought is in nowise offered as a thesis,
the author's meaning is clear: Paulo Honório is neither admirable
nor despicable; he is simply the product of the cruel social and
economic realities of the Northeast. Paulo places the blame not
on himself but on the world of the Northeast: "It was this way
of life that made me worthless."[31] We are reminded of the violence of Viçosa, the "hardhearted landholders," and the severity
of Ramos' own father as factors that helped to form Paulo Honório.

Descriptions of nature are sparingly used: the hostile landscape limits and blights the lives of the characters, and has no
other meaning. Paulo Honório appreciates its beauty only because the cotton fields, the red-backed cattle, and the green forests
are his property. Only the sight of the land can stir a spark of
aesthetic appreciation in him; then he can declare, "I became convinced that this is not a bad world."[32]

In *St. Bernard* Graciliano Ramos most directly enunciates his
aesthetic views, based on absolute honesty in communicating
thought and feeling. Though satirically expressed, a central
opinion is well shown in the scene which takes place after Paulo
has decided to write a novel in collaboration with his friends the
priest, the lawyer, and the newspaperman.

The result was disaster. Two weeks after our first meeting, the editor
of the *Cruzeiro* presented me with two typewritten chapters, so full of
stupidities that I got mad:
"Go to hell, Gondim. You fouled up everything. This is too high-
falutin', it's awful, it's idiotic. Nobody in God's world talks like that!"
Azevedo Gondim extinguished his smile, gulped, picked up the pieces

of his small vanity, and replied with vexation that an artist cannot write as he talks.

"He can't?" I asked in amazement. "Why not?"

Azevedo Gondim replied that he cannot because he cannot.

"That's why it's written as it is. Literature is literature, Seu Paulo. People discuss, quarrel, conduct business naturally, but putting words down on paper is something else again. If I set out to write as I speak, no one would read me."[33]

Paulo Honório will not write that kind of novel. He abandons his collaborators and begins his book with the request, "Those who read me will please be kind enough . . . to translate this into literary language, if they care to."[34]

With *Anguish* (*Angústia*) Ramos carries the Brazilian novel to a stage beyond that reached by Machado de Assis. In his effort to capture as much of the human essence as possible, Ramos adapts the so-called interior monologue to the study of an individual Northeasterner, Luis Silva, whose existence is endowed with sociological as well as psychological meaning. The full impact of the social criticism in *Anguish* is felt only after a second or third reading. Lest it be forgotten, this is the novel that Ramos wrote during the period of his political persecution and imprisonment.

Anguish is the history of the mind of Luis Silva, which has been scarred by depressing childhood experiences; which has registered impressions, sometimes vague, of thirst in the sertão, of a brave and respected grandfather whose fazenda had gradually gone to ruin, of a father who died when Luis was a boy and whose death cannot be forgotten; and which can call up the image of Seu Evaristo, after he hanged himself, or of the amiable José Bahia, his grandfather's bodyguard hired on occasion to do murder. Luis Silva's mind has recorded more—his life at school as a small boy in a backlands town, his education in Maceió, his "gypsy's life" as a poor schoolteacher, moving on when he had taught all that he himself had been taught, his rounds as a beggar, a "hitch" in the army, and a period in jail for his political beliefs. After the collapse of his grandfather's holdings in the sertão, Luis Silva painfully attempts to eke out an existence in the society of the littoral. Overcome by misery and frustration, he ends in a dingy little room in Maceió, where, as a petty bureaucrat, he writes "what he is told to write." Ungovernable forces of sex complete the destruction.

The harried Luis Silva has never known real love, although he has purchased its facsimile, until he glimpses Marina, the girl next door on a shabby street in Maceió. At first promising to marry him, she leaves him because he is poor, and transfers her affections to a well-to-do young lawyer of the upper class, Julião Tavares. Tavares seduces the girl and abandons her when she becomes pregnant. Luis Silva's jealousy now turns to rage. In this crisis, the past, the figure of his proud and dignified old grandfather, the image of men violently dying in the sertão, of the killer José Bahia, of a snake coiled around a man's neck, of the swelling abdomen of Marina, of a rope—the ineluctable past merges in the unbearable present. His mind unhinged, Luis Silva strangles Julião Tavares, and the final pages of the novel, reminiscent of Molly Bloom's soliloquy, reveal the nature of Luis Silva's madness.

Only after the novel is finished does the reader realize that the entire story has been related by a man out of his mind. There are two levels of action: in one, Luis Silva narrates the love affair with Marina; in the other, past and present, memories, fears, and speculations are interwoven and at last chaotically confused. The account thus gains the eerie quality of a dream, or of delirium, which is unparalleled in the Brazilian novel.

The anguish of Luis Silva is the result of his thwarted sexual desire for Marina. This is made clear in page after page of morbid eroticism, in which the man's instinctive urges are shown compressed within him like a spring. His crime against Tavares was motivated by defeated love and by accompanying jealousy and wrath. However, Luis Silva's mind was already in a precarious state, weakened by years of privation and despair.

Another sharper kind of anguish in the novel is that of Graciliano Ramos himself, surveying the unfortunate and apparently irremediable social and economic conditions of his Northeast. The novel's high social sense is found in its representation of the degrading conditions of life of the masses—the Marinas and the Luis Silvas, victims of an unjust organization of society, scourged from the sertão, like Luis Silva, to be crushed by civilization, to be coerced, like Marina, by a wealthy Julião Tavares, or to be reduced, like Dona Adélia, the pathetic mother of Marina, to "a piece of filthy rag."[135] None of these characters is shown as courageous or virtuous, as might be the heroes of a Jorge Amado. Curiously, not even Julião Tavares is blackened. "Marina was an instrument and deserved compassion. Dona Adélia was an instrument and deserved compassion. Julião Tavares was also an instrument, but I did not feel sorry for him. I felt the same hatred, now increased, that he has always inspired in me."[136]

Does the author mean to equate the oppressed and the oppressor? Jorge Amado would have made it clear that Marina was a victim and that Tavares was a culprit. Does Ramos, seeing farther than Amado, find them both innocent? Or both guilty? Or is he indifferent to their fate? Is something called "civilization" responsible for their misery? The novelist never made clear his attitude toward society and its organization. It is as if this aspect of his writing had purposely been obscured.

Ever since *St. Bernard* this much, at least, of the novelist's meaning has been clear: the struggle for existence in the littoral is so desperate that the individual must, as did Paulo Honório, sell his soul in order to survive. In Luis Silva, Álvaro Lins sees a character who, "in a certain sense, represents the other side of Paulo Honório."[137] Paulo Honório has conquered his environment; Luis Silva has succumbed to his. To Ramos, life in the agricultural and relatively Europeanized belt of the coastland is untempered hell, whether one prospers, as does Paulo Honório, or perishes, as does Luis Silva.

Throughout his works, with the exception of the somewhat unrepresentative *Caetés,* the novelist juxtaposes "sertão" and "civilization" in a remarkable way. We are reminded of Euclydes da Cunha, who called attention to the chasm between sertanejo society and the European-type communities of the littoral.

The one character who is unsoiled by contact with the coastal society is the cowherd Fabiano of *Parched Lives* (*Vidas Secas*). It is meaningful that Fabiano, because he has remained apart from civilization, is the purest and most tranquil of the novelist's creatures. Through Fabiano, Victória, and the boys—not to mention the dog Baleia—the author of *Parched Lives* has translated into human terms the tragedy of life as it must be lived in the sertão, the skills of the vaqueiro upon which livelihood depends, the physical conditions of existence under the threat of the great climatic monster at whose whim all live, flee, or die—the periodic seca. Spare in action, the novel concentrates upon Fabiano and his family, who, scourged by the drought, take refuge in an abandoned ranch house, and at last are saved by the rains. Later the deadly seca again sets them loose on the barren sertão.

Fabiano is wise in the ways of taming wild horses, of tracking cattle in the underbrush of the spiny caatinga, of curing their diseases. He knows how to survive and to take care of his wife Sinha Victória and the two boys. His ignorance is that of the man raised in the wilderness.

He lived far from men and got along well only with animals. His hard feet broke thorns and did not feel the heat of the ground. When mounted, he became one with his horse, glued to him. He spoke a sing-song language, a monosyllabic and guttural language that his companion understood. On foot, he had trouble walking. He leaned first to one side, then to the other, clumsy, stooped, and ugly. At times, in his relations with people, he used the same language which he would address to the animals—exclamations, onomatopoeias. In truth he spoke little. He admired the long and difficult words of city people, tried in vain to reproduce some of them, but he knew they were useless and perhaps dangerous.[38]

Civilization is represented by the distant town to which Fabiano made infrequent trips—to church once a year because he "had religion"; to the business office of the fazendeiro to settle accounts and perhaps be cheated because he could not read or add; to the store where he procured supplies. In town the risks that lay in wait for him were the saloon, with its rum and gambling, and the "yellow soldier" (yellow, presumably from worms or malaria), who, representing the abstraction "government," teased him and stepped on his sandaled toes with heavy boots.

Fabiano is not ambitious for himself. His aim is to teach his boys to be like him, as he is like his own father and grandfather before him. He knows he must work for others and, like a cabra, "keep his place."

All right. He was born with his destiny, no one was to blame for his having been born with an evil destiny. What could he do? Could he change fate? If someone had told him he could improve his situation, he would have been amazed. He had come into this world to break animals, cure their sores with prayers, mend fences from wet season to dry. . . . He accepted it, he didn't ask for anything more. If they gave him what was his, it was fine. They didn't. He was out of luck, he was like a dog, he got only the bones. Why was it that rich men still kept taking some of the bones away from him? It even made you sick at your stomach the way important people bothered about such trifles.[39]

Significant are the closing words of *Parched Lives*, for they explain much not only about Paulo Honório and Luis Silva but also about Ramos himself. As Fabiano and Victória are forced from the backlands and head for the coast, their thoughts and fresh hopes turn to the *mata,* the well-watered farming belt, where lie the possibilities of improving the sertanejo's hard lot. "The children in schools, learning difficult and necessary matters. They themselves, two little old people, finishing up like dogs . . . What could they do? Fearfully, they slowed their pace. They would reach an unknown, civilized land and would be held fast in it. And the sertão would continue to send people there. The sertão would send to the city strong, brutish men like Fabiano, Sinha Victória and the two boys."[40]

Structurally, *Parched Lives* differs from the well-made nineteenth-century novel typified by *Caetés;* from the autobiographical novel represented by *St. Bernard;* and from *Anguish,* which in form derives from modern stream-of-consciousness writing. Ramos' last novel is related entirely in the third person. There is scarcely a word of dialogue, and Fabiano and Sinha Victória are brought to life through the narration of an artist who appears to be endowed with the same temperament as his characters. Thus is created the impression of the novelist's profound understanding of sertanejo psychology.

Parched Lives is made up of disconnected scenes. Each chapter (some examples are "Moving," "Baleia," "The Jail," "Fabiano," "Holiday," "Flight") has its own unity, its own near-independence, and might be said to constitute a short story, in which action is less important than the study of the psychological make-up of the character, even though it be the dog Baleia, whose death is described in one of the most moving chapters in all of modern Brazilian literature. The novelist himself has said that *Parched Lives* grew out of a short story, "Baleia," based upon the death of a pet dog that he had seen his grandfather kill. The story was published and well received, and he later returned to the subject of Fabiano and elaborated it into a novel.[41] We may speculate that Ramos found in the short-story form the literary vehicle that best suited him. All his writings since *Anguish* have taken that form—even his autobiography *Childhood,* certain chapters of which have been published separately.[42] In less than two hundred pages, *Parched Lives* reveals more about life in the sertão than several thousand pages of sociological treatises could reveal. This book, which is both regional and universal, equals Ramos' earlier masterpieces *St. Bernard* and *Anguish.*

Rich in psychological revelations of the human soul and in sociological meaning, the novels of Ramos are esteemed also for their literary style. As Osório Borba has described it, Ramos writes as he talks, "an erudite version of the countryman's dialect of the Northeast, regionalism in classic form, slang of the zone and plebeian 'cuss words' carefully set down in the purest of Portuguese, with pronouns rigorously placed and exact grammatical usage."[43] Using language perfectly in accord with the theme, the characters, and the locale, Ramos achieves an artistic form which is incomparable in its sobriety, elegance, and refinement. And although his language is not notable for poetic effect, it has what might be called a Parnassian beauty. Strange that it has also been called "uncouth," "arid," "dry," "barren," and even "too highly refined." But as Guilherme de Figueiredo has said: "The constant polishing of his style, so far from robbing it of its effects, lends astounding force to a mere sentence, to a mere word. He writes almost mathematically: his expressions are immutable within their framework."[44] With Ramos, language is a precision tool with which effects hitherto unrecorded in Brazilian literature have been made possible.

That his style and, indeed, every detail of the novel are the result of continual purification is illustrated by the fact that *St. Bernard* was thrice written before its final form was attained.[45] We have reason to suspect that the choice of an adjective may have caused Ramos "to sweat in agony," as has been said of Flaubert. The purifying process accounts for the fact that Ramos' novels and short stories are few in number and contain such richness within reduced dimensions. The four slender volumes of prose may prove to be the most solid achievement in the field of the modern Brazilian novel.

CHAPTER V

RACHEL DE QUEIROZ

Rachel de Queiroz

THE NOVEL of the Northeast benefits much from the fact that Rachel de Queiroz is a woman. Through her the novel gains an extra dimension, as it were, an insight into feminine psychology to which readers of the Brazilian novel are little accustomed. Certainly no other writer of the Northeast shows so great an understanding of maternal instinct and tenderness toward children, and, above all, so warm and generous a spirit toward all mankind. Strange that at the same time she should be capable of a literary realism so dispassionate as to be called "virile" by certain Brazilian critics.

Rachel de Queiroz was born in the seaport town of Fortaleza, not far from the equator, on November 17, 1910. Early she was taken inland to be reared on her father's ranch in the sertão. There life still flowed in the old patriarchal way, with a little community of Negroes, mestizos, mulattoes, and caboclos, some of them former slaves, all incorporated into the social and economic life at the ranch of the white fazendeiro. She had to fit into the pattern which had been established for hundreds of years in this part of Brazil: she must be cloistered and submissive in a world dominated by men. This fact is important, for it helps to explain certain attitudes of the novelist, or better, of her characters who, as women, rebel against their traditional status.

135

In Rachel's part of Ceará, the arid but potentially productive sertão, they have a saying, "The land is good. All it needs is rain." In visualizing her ranch home high on a bald hill overlooking the countryside, we should not miss the detail of the life-giving reservoir flanking the Big House. Its rain water often made the difference between life and death. The crucial experience of her childhood was the drought of 1915, when that reservoir and all the surrounding territory went dry. Much of the backland population was forced to migrate to the thin green line of the coast. Families disintegrated, herds were turned free to forage and die, bones both animal and human strewed the dusty roads to Fortaleza. The ravages of the drought of 1915 lasted for years after the return of the rains. And, like the land, the mind of Rachel de Queiroz still carried the imprint of that tragic time when, years later, she wrote *The Year Fifteen*.

The family took a trip to Rio de Janeiro in order to forget the horrors of this experience.[1] Then, in Fortaleza, Rachel attended a convent school, undoubtedly the model for the unforgettable "golden cage" of *Three Marias*. This was a period of wide reading and intellectual awakening. Her precocious literary urges need not surprise us. Ceará has stout literary heroes and traditions in the novelists José de Alencar and Domingos Olympio, the critic Araripe Júnior, and the philosopher Farias Brito. And Rachel had an added incentive to choose a career of letters—the fact that her family was related to both Araripe Júnior and Alencar.[2] Thus the phenomenon of a cultured and talented young girl writing a novel in the remoteness of Ceará has at least a partial explanation.

At the early age of fifteen, Rachel had completed her training to be an elementary school teacher. The five years before the publication of her first novel were spent in teaching and in literary and journalistic writing in Ceará. All the lines of her previous experience seemed to converge when in 1930 she published *The Year Fifteen*.

After this book, which established her reputation, Rachel de Queiroz published three novels, *John Michael* (1932), *Stony Road* (1937), and *Three Marias* (1939), each of which further confirmed her artistic talent. Since 1939 her literary activity has been confined to translating English, Russian, German, French, and Spanish authors for the Brazilian public and, since the early 'forties, to writing a weekly column (*rodapé*) in the literary supplements of various Rio de Janeiro newspapers and magazines.

In recent years Rachel de Queiroz has lived quietly with her husband on a shady street of Governor's Island in the Bay of Rio de Janeiro. Biographers have gallantly respected the novelist's wish for privacy; most of the pertinent details about Rachel's temperament and literary personality must be gleaned from her own writings, above all from *The Damsel and the Cross-Eyed Mooress* (*A Donzela e a Moura Torta*), a recently published collection of reminiscences, "profiles" of interesting people, and impressionistic essays on the passing scene in Rio de Janeiro and the nation at large. In this really good document on Rachel de Queiroz, not only do we get a glimpse of the author as a young girl, but also we learn something of her literary personality and her attitudes. Her political opinions are few; they show contempt for Fascist dictators in Europe, through whom, perhaps, she is expressing in the only way possible her aversion for despots of the Brazilian variety. In one article, "Old Jovino," Rachel admires a gaunt old Brazilian Communist of the early 'thirties who, despite privation and punishment, maintained his political heresy. Jovino is not a co-religionist of the author, but she does recognize in him certain admirable traits, particularly the one she seems most to prize, fierce resistance to evil destiny.

The frustrated biographer of Rachel de Queiroz turns with delight to *The Damsel and the Cross-Eyed Mooress,* for from it emerges a real personality merely guessed at in the novels. The pervading sentiment of these well-turned prose bits is her compassion for humanity, which here is expressed in several articles about soldiers of the Brazilian Expeditionary Force. Rachel laments that she is "a woman without a son to become a soldier, a worker, or a voter."[3] She is tormented by the fact that she is childless, personally incomplete. Her novels are preoccupied with the theme of maternal love, at times triumphant but more often sadly thwarted. The tenderness she is prevented from showing to a child of her own is given to men and women and children everywhere with a sincerity and reserve that save her from the charge of sentimentality.

Rachel's affection for the Northeast, for Ceará, for the sertão, and her fervent wish to return are also revealed in *The Damsel and the Cross-Eyed Mooress.* Despite her wide culture and nearly twenty years of living away from her home country, she has never lost the "dust of the province" that hangs upon her and her writing. Her universality has its tap roots in the Northeast.

It was almost inevitable that Rachel de Queiroz should begin her career with a sociological novel. The time was charged with the spirit of change—political, social, literary. A revolution was brewing; the need for social reform was widespread; and a new and successful departure had been taken by the Brazilian novel with the publication of José Américo de Almeida's *Cane-Trash.* In those unpleasant days, literature gave the idealistic writer the chance to do something about conditions that were, to a sensitive soul, virtually unbearable. These factors unquestionably influenced Rachel in her literary debut with *The Year Fifteen (O Quinze).*[4]

The theme of calamitous drought in the Northeast is old, and "drought literature," as it has been called,[5] is an original characteristic of Brazilian literature. From Rachel's first work, with its mournful theme of drought and desolation, we might have expected something girlish and melodramatic. But in *The Year Fifteen,* dead seriousness (but not sentimentality) sets the keynote of the narrative. The romance of Conceição and Vicente, likewise, is characterized by gravity and thoughtfulness (but not dullness).

In this work, which undertook to combine the two themes of cyclic drought and of woman's social role, Rachel encountered certain novelistic problems which she was later to solve. Of these the chief may well have been how to give social breadth and significance and, at the same time, human drama to the tragedy of the cowherd Chico Bento and his family. The most striking defect of the novel is the author's restricted view. The reader is regrettably left with the impression that the drought was a personal affliction wreaked upon the poor cowherd by Heaven, for Rachel never quite manages to convey the extent of the disaster that drought brings to hundreds of thousands of sertanejos.

Unlike Américo's *Cane-Trash, The Year Fifteen* is devoid of pleading, and reveals only the harsh facts concerning the drought. The scene is the ranching community of Quixadá, Ceará; the central action is the migration of sertanejos from the area, forced by one of the worst of the periodic droughts that still afflict the area. No answer for the problem is suggested. Rachel merely concentrates upon the human suffering that accompanies these natural phenomena.

Because of the drought, Chico Bento's employer turns his skinny cattle loose to shift for themselves in the ashen, sun-drenched caatinga. To find work, the cowherd, his wife, and six children are forced to go afoot the hundred miles of desert to the coast. Food and water are soon exhausted. One child dies from eating a poisonous root; another is lost; the eldest, a girl, seeks work in a village along the route and becomes a prostitute; the youngest lad nearly dies of hunger and disease.

Along the trail of Chico Bento, against the bare landscape, Rachel de Queiroz looks unflinchingly at scenes of hunger, thirst, fatigue, and death. An example of her artistry is the description of the little band at the end of a hard day's march, so starved that all walk with a drunken lurch.

The setting sun, flaming, intensely red, was, like a drowning man, sinking on the near-by horizon.

The reeling shadows lengthened along the strip of red-brown road, which stretched over the top of a rocky hill and disappeared among the houses of a sleepy roadside community.

Overcome by misery and despair, the shadows dragged their feet unconsciously, in the final, drunken stage of hunger.

The slender outline of a woman knelt on the red earth.

A parched figure squatted down beside her and plunged his weary head between his bony knees, supporting it with his hands.

Only one young boy, standing apart, looked thoughtfully at the group, crouched in weakness and fatigue.

His pained voice called to them with hopeful words.

And his hand could be seen in the deepening darkness of the afternoon, pointing to a cluster of houses, farther on.

But the only sign of life in the motionless group was the soft intermittent crying of a child.[6]

Through the use of a distant perspective, the eye seizes upon major objects—the sun, the red-brown strip of road, the deepening shadows in which human figures become almost indistinguishable as mere staggering outlines. Figurative language, the stumbling block of José Américo de Almeida in his version of the drought novel, is kept at a minimum. A hell-on-earth atmosphere is created by the use of a few details, and emotion, in this agonizing glimpse, is held tightly controlled.

Knowing, however, that the reader can stand only so much horror, the novelist interleaves with the grim story of the retirantes the romance of Vicente and Conceição, to which the tragedy of drought seems to communicate some of its harshness and aridity. The effect, fortunately, is to make a novel of what might have been merely documentary.

Vicente has decided to endure the drought in the sertão. Absorbed in his efforts to save his herd, and too shy to declare his love to his sweetheart, he sees Conceição return to Fortaleza, where she teaches school and where she helps to care for the refugees flocking to the capital. Here she finds what is left of the family of Chico Bento, whose youngest son is her godchild.

Before they leave for São Paulo, their "promised land," the parents allow her to adopt the sickly boy. Upon him Conceição lavishes her irrepressible maternal affections—she is destined never to be Vicente's wife.

The love affair of Vicente and Conceição is destroyed by the sexual code of the backland Northeast. According to custom, the woman is strictly cloistered both before and after marriage. For the man, on the contrary, extramarital promiscuity is permitted and sometimes even encouraged.

The theme of this sexual drama is stated unequivocally by Gilberto Freyre in his masterly study of the historical basis of the formation of the Brazilian family, *The Masters and the Slaves*. Another sociologist, examining the Northeastern pattern, which is common also in the rest of Brazil, notes that it is being changed under the triple force of immigration, industrialization, and urbanization. Now the Brazilian woman is beginning to enjoy more freedom and a status "nearer that of men."[7] In the novels of Rachel de Queiroz the central feminine characters are constantly protesting through their actions the almost Oriental submissiveness required of women in that society, in which the author herself was reared.

Because of a rumor, tragically unfounded, that Vicente has sown wild oats in the accepted way, Conceição displays a coolness toward the young man that is fatal to their romance. She is urged by her mild-tempered old grandmother, Dona Inácia, who has reared the girl in the sertão, to give in to the older standards: "But my child, that happens to all of them. White men, in the sertão—you always hear that kind of story. Anyway, she's not a Negress—she's a light-skinned mestizo girl." And she reveals that she had once been similarly resentful and rebellious, but "it is all quite natural and to be expected, and we have to get used to it."[8]

The status of woman in society is of particular concern to Rachel. In none of her first four novels is this interest lacking.

Conceição, who cannot accept her traditional role, is merely a preliminary sketch of the feminine type Rachel portrayed with notable success in two later novels. Conceição cannot stand as a finished psychological study; rather is she important as a symbol of the new woman in Brazil. Independent, she is quick to challenge society in the name of her personal freedom and dignity.

Maternal love is another preoccupation of the novelist. And just as the symbol of the modern woman is taking shape in Rachel's thinking, so does she seem to be formulating, in *The Year Fifteen*, her ideas of mother love and the importance of the instinctive or biological aspect of her characters. Destiny has decreed that Conceição shall not fall in love, and her decision to "walk alone," as she expresses it, is a sacrifice, for, "after all, woman's true destiny is to cradle a child at her breast."[9] In foregoing marriage and agreeing to rear Chico Bento's child, she is bending her will to that of society and is channeling within socially acceptable limits her impulse to motherhood.

In her first two novels Rachel is so absorbed with sociological themes that she does no more than broach a subject that becomes her central interest in later work. That is her intense preoccupation with love. In the light of *Stony Road* and *Three Marias*, the compromise of Conceição with society can no longer be considered a satisfactory solution to the problem of being an unmarried woman in the society of the Northeast. The implications of these two novels are for women not only of Brazil but everywhere—women who are capable of unusual heroism and integrity.

The role of women in *John Michael (João Miguel)*,[10] Rachel's second novel, is a reflex of the central social study of João Miguel, a mestizo murderer incarcerated in a little jail in the sertão community of Baturité, Ceará. The prisoner's common-law wife Santa is a prostitute whom Rachel analyzes with a deep compassion that recalls Amando Fontes' warm and dignified treatment of such public women in his *Siriry Street.* In Brazil, where for certain reasons prostitution is "a general phenomenon and fully accepted by the family and by the authorities,"[11] modern novelists have not failed to sense the tragic human loss involved.

Rachel's characterization of these women who live by their bodies is done with artistic imagination as well as understanding. Particularly noteworthy is her method of revealing Santa, not by her own statements or actions (she is an infrequent visitor to the jail) but through statements made about her by the prostitute Filó, who with seeming optimism accepts her own vile status and reproves Santa for her refusal to do likewise: "She thought she was too good, she did not want to be like us, she said she would not hire herself out to a man. She might take a lover, but it was going to be like a marriage. For love and for esteem . . . No sir, not for money. Well, tongues wagged and she got caught. People who put on too many airs end up worse than the rest . . ."[12] Santa did take another lover when João Miguel was arrested and jailed. But that was "fate," the sertanejo's eternal explanation for the unknowable. And Santa continued to visit João Miguel, though she would not hurt him with the admission that the jailer Salu was her new man.

Again, as in *The Year Fifteen,* Rachel is concerned with woman's place in the scheme of things which perpetuates the sexual relationship between white master and Negro or mestizo slave. Filó, a Negress reared in a Big House kitchen, is an unhappy symbol of that relationship and its present-day social result. The birth of her mulatto child caused her to be "set loose in the world" when she was fifteen. The crime of this woman, who is the prison cook and the concubine of Seu Doca, one of the jailers, is stated with the novelist's characteristic succinctness: "a drunken argument, a razor, and a poor devil down under the table with his guts slashed."[13] Not much different is the situation of Maria Elói, who is raising her two children in the cell with her.

Rachel focuses upon the warmly human, the universally understandable qualities of her subjects. Despite their degradation, some of the prisoners are seen as persons of worth, and none is viewed as an "enemy of society." Although most of them are Negroes or caboclos, an important exception is Colonel Nonato, a respected old gentleman, white, of course, who never would have been imprisoned for murder except that he was an enemy of the political party in power. As Rachel de Queiroz sees it, there is truth in João Miguel's assertion: "In my mind, this world belongs to those who can do something about it. Those who suffer in it are the ones who do not have the ability to be somebody big. Punishment would be a good thing if it were for everybody. But the big shots, who pay dogs like us to kill whomever they please—did you ever see one of them get even a taste of jail?"[14] The note of outspoken social protest here is a rare, almost jarring sound. Rachel usually avoids the soapbox novel. She represents her characters with objectivity, and their histories speak more eloquently than indictments.

The reader gets the impression that because these sertanejos are docile and obedient to their destiny, the little jail at Baturité will continue to house such men and women, who have known every sorrow but death. And destiny means poverty, illiteracy, disease, and malnutrition among the masses, who are separated by an enormous social gap from their upper-class masters.

The first few hours of João Miguel's imprisonment, after he has stabbed another caboclo in a tavern brawl, show him in various stages emerging from drunkenness: irritation at the raucous singing from a near-by cell, later embarrassment, and finally shame as, after the effects of alcohol wear off, he realizes the nature of his crime. In succeeding days Rachel records his self-consciousness in the presence of his fellow inmates until he learns that they do not regard him as a heinous criminal. On the contrary, the prisoners who have taken a life feel themselves morally superior to those who are merely thieves!

In a matter of months João Miguel becomes resigned to his new situation. However, he never stops asking his jailers when he will be brought to trial. Eventually he is found innocent, and prepares to resume his old life, "renting his arms from door to door, from one piece of ground to the next, without being able to call his own even the hoe with which he dug the earth, the axe with which he cut the wood . . ."[15] A free man now, he nevertheless spends a final night in jail—one more instance of detail happily chosen to document the confusion new freedom brings to his mind—and then sets out for the unpromising future.

He looked at the landscape around him.

The earth, at his feet, was like a dazzling promise. And his return to the blessed loveliness of the world was like a resurrection.

At that moment, at least, all was behind him: the past, the crime, the suffering, and the regret for what he had irrevocably lost. And the hunger, the misery, all the future ills, the prospect of which had so tormented the sleepless hours of the night preceding, vanished like a light mist, like the cloud bank which, only a moment ago covering a purple segment of the mountains, had now disappeared.

He was living only in this happy hour of freedom. And his chest breathed deeply the fragrant air which came from the fresh earth, as from an enormous bed of roses.[16]

How has Rachel bridged the enormous gap between herself and the wreched little murderer? Through love for her fellow man, which underlies everything she writes. Out of this love, in combination with her fine talent for observing the key details of human behavior, flows the understanding that makes possible such character studies. João Miguel takes on universal qualities as a result of the author's psychological penetration. The novel is much more than a sociological case study of a prisoner, or a probing analysis of human detritus. At its highest level, *John Michael* is a symbolic affirmation of one of Rachel's most cherished convictions—that men of all conditions, and particularly the lowly, must face their destiny, no matter how unpromising, with the resolute spirit of free men.

Five changeful years elapsed between Rachel's second and third novels. Powerful factors that in the early 'thirties influenced the social content of her first books no longer operated. A new element of thoughtfulness gives an almost philosophical quality to *Stony Road (Caminho de Pedras)*,[17] whose central theme is womanly love. The topic had been broached in the arid romance of Vicente and Conceição, as well as in the socially less acceptable loves of Santa, the prostitute. In the present novel, however, sociological considerations are dominated by the love theme, and the emotional content is more intense.

When *Stony Road* appeared in 1937, its reception was in certain quarters far different from the friendly treatment accorded Rachel's earlier novels.[18] It was not difficult to interpret the work as an attack upon the institution of marriage; and, with its sympathetic regard for men and women engaged in a controversial political action, it could appear to the undiscerning as one more propagandistic tract. True, it does revolve around a group of radical labor organizers, but it is not a proletarian novel of the type written by Jorge Amado. Political discussions, meetings of agitators, and police raids are only the background for a drama that far transcends the political.

Almir de Andrade has brilliantly set forth the real character of the novelist's thought as it is reflected in the conduct of Noemi, the heroine of *Stony Road,* who, he notes, does not seek to revolutionize the bases of society but rather is motivated by the need to be sincere with herself. Noemi obviously is no sordid nymphomaniac: her motives are pure, "of a purity that men and the world do not understand, because it dwells in deep regions where only the minds and hearts of the free may enter."[19]

Noemi is led down new avenues of thought and becomes aware of the "possibilities of freedom" as a result of participation in one of the flourishing labor movements of the era. "She was now a free spirit, hearing the story of other free spirits. She had fled her habitual center of gravity, she had lost the notion of 'our daily bread.' At that moment nothing was either moral or immoral, nothing was forbidden or permitted; there was no time, there was no space: only the intoxication of the moment in which were revealed the possibilities of freedom."[20]

The idealistic nature of Rachel's philosophy is shown in the character of Noemi's husband, a white-collar worker in Fortaleza. The novelist has represented João Jacques not as a wife-beater, drunkard, or philanderer but as a decent sort, whom Noemi happens not to love. When she falls in love with Roberto, a young labor organizer, the triangle is closed. The chief obstacle to a separation is a little boy, Guri, whom both parents adore, and Noemi cannot bring herself to discuss a parting with her husband: "You do not understand how difficult it is for me to speak to him. He is good, he is sincere. He is crazy about his son. He has never deceived me. Ten times I have tried to tell him. When I am about to speak to him, I cannot . . ."[21] Noemi wishes to proceed with decency, to avoid a mere liaison with Roberto; furthermore, she is not convinced that the pursuit of her own happiness justifies the probable injury to João Jacques. When Noemi succumbs to fleshly desire, her disdained husband leaves his house and child. The full weight of social disapproval falls upon Noemi. Roberto, significantly, is not much scorned—in men, Brazilians are used to such behavior.

An incidental aspect of *Stony Road* is its implicit satire of a kind of modern marriage maintained for mere appearance after love has vanished. To accept the hypocrisy of such a marriage would have been the easier course for Noemi. In contrast to Conceição, of *The Year Fifteen,* who was willing to compromise, Noemi challenges social convention in her decision to live with Roberto.

Not even the most tragic misfortunes can dismay her, although she is well-nigh overwhelmed by the sickness and death of her little son Guri. Only the thought of Roberto's unborn child and her indomitable will sustain her. To Noemi, "love justifies all things," and she steadfastly remains with Roberto.

The scene of Guri's death is surely one of the high points in modern Brazilian literature.

At noon the doctor left and went to lunch. He said the case was very delicate.

In the afternoon everything seemed to go better.

That night the nightmare began again.

Beside the bed the doctor, motionless, stood watch; in an abrupt voice he ordered a sponge-bath, more blankets. Noemi's hands, arms, body, eyes worked, obeyed. Before daybreak the doctor went away. He returned in the early morning. Shortly thereafter came another attack, the strongest of all, and Guri died.

Death is silent and modest. It is the living who cover it with wailing, confusion, and rites. Guri died softly, without speaking, without knowing, certainly without any regret. He merely opened his mouth, gasped air with greater anguish than before, and a yellow tide surged gradually through his body, beneath his skin, reaching his fever-flushed cheeks, gaining his mouth, his forehead, his fingers. That was all. The doctor said quietly: "This is the end."[22]

When Noemi is given an assignment to distribute illegal propaganda leaflets, Roberto insists on accompanying her. They are surprised by the police, and Roberto is arrested. "One took hold of Noemi's arm, another, of Roberto's. And the third, the one with the revolver, silently took the package that each was clutching to himself."[23] The scene, beautifully told, reveals the spirituality of a love which society had considered carnal.

Stony Road may be considered a preliminary sketch of the social and moral question of love beyond society's barriers. Noemi's motivation in defying convention is rather vague, but this minor weakness is remedied in Rachel de Queiroz' fourth novel, *Three Marias* (*As Três Marias*). Instead of showing merely one crisis in the life of its protagonist, Rachel gives a more complete account of the central figure, Guta. She describes the conflict that arises when a powerful and independent personality comes in contact with the social restrictions placed on the urge to love, to make a home, to have children. In this psychological study the novelist attempts to face some of life's gravest problems—the nature of society, of God, of good and evil—as observed in the mind of a lonely, sensitive, and contemplative young woman. Through various stages of thinking and feeling, Guta is followed from childhood to womanhood. At last, when she defies society, her character and reasons are clearly understandable.

A third of the novel deals with life in a convent boarding school for girls in Fortaleza, where the three Marias—Maria Augusta or Guta, Maria Glória, Maria José—all from broken homes, are sent to receive their secondary education. The convent nuns, who are like "wax dolls," are pointedly contrasted with the young girls, whose fresh animality their guardians are at times powerless to curb. The theme of love in this artificial atmosphere takes the form of romantic idyl: Maria Glória meets a young lad on one of her rare trips to the outside and, as a consequence, the other two Marias participate in her emotional reactions.

Not only does Rachel examine the entwining lives of the three Marias, but also she widens her view of society by dwelling upon the character and personal history of many of their schoolmates. The social stratification which exists outside the convent is echoed within the walls by the nuns' segregation of the orphans "because they were the poor of the earth and were learning properly to live and to suffer like the poor."[24] Social injustice is made palpable to Guta in the person of Jandira, a mestizo girl who is stigmatized not because of her mixed blood but because of her illegitimate birth—an important sociological note in this novel.

The threads of the lives of the girls after their graduation are dexterously woven into the subsequent narration. Rachel de Queiroz concentrates upon Guta and her development from a schoolgirl dependent upon her father and stepmother, who live in the far sertão, into a thoughtful young woman making her own way in the city of Fortaleza. As might be expected, Rachel is centrally concerned with Guta's aspirations to love. At first the young girl is merely curious about this passion, which she has never experienced. Then she becomes enamored of a graying artist, a married man, for whom her attachment is only spiritual; "For me . . . Raul represented love, and as such it was pure, intangible, above all and everyone, above good and evil."[25] Guta suffers painful disillusionment when she discovers that the man expects her to become his mistress, and quickly terminates this relationship.

Later she unwittingly becomes involved in the suicide of a friend, Aluízio. He takes poison and Guta is summoned to his bedside to be charged by relatives with responsibility for his death. Until this moment she had been given no inkling of the shy Aluízio's feelings.

After this ugly joke of fate, Guta travels to Rio de Janeiro and meets a Jewish refugee, Isaac. Asking nothing, expecting nothing, the girl for the first time knows the beauty of love. Isaac, however, is poor and is faced with possible deportation. After Guta has returned alone to Fortaleza, she decides to destroy Isaac's unborn child—the greatest sacrifice she could make—and spends a frenzied night on the jolting, bruising rides at an amusement park. There a drunken man, watching the thrilling "whip," which passes so close it frightens him, mutters to himself, "That's a crime!" Rachel de Queiroz, in thus introducing the word, although in a different context, is aware that society will call Guta's act by that name. The novelist makes it clear, however, in artistically integrated scenes of suffering children, that a greater "crime" would be to allow a child to come into the world to be the victim of a vengeful society that would not forgive its illegitimate birth.

The progression of Rachel's thought thus becomes evident; from Conceição, who in compromise would accept another woman's child to rear; through Noemi, who to have her lover's child was willing to challenge social usage; and now to Guta, who shows what the novelist considers the supreme form of heroism. She desires a child as much as does Noemi and is as willing to incur society's displeasure to have it. A new consideration gives her pause, however—the thought of what the unborn child may have to face in a hostile society. Therefore, Guta's "criminal" act stands, in Rachel's scale of values, above any other in the series of novels: out of compassion for her child, which transcends even love, Guta destroys the symbol of love. In the thinking of Rachel de Queiroz, humanitarian love comes before the physical (and "spiritual") love of man and woman for each other.

In addition to probing the fastnesses of Guta's mind, the novelist proceeds to examine social values in a critical spirit. Her reflections upon good and evil are brought out through Maria José, who, after leaving school, sublimates her fleshly desires in a sort of mystic devotion to Catholicism. It is she who censures Guta for her failure to feel remorse or fear, in the religious sense, for her transgression of the moral code. Maria José also condemns her own father for abandoning his frowsy wife in search of love elsewhere. And Guta, questioning always, thinks to herself: "Even your father's great sin—is it really a sin? You look upon him as a reprobate, and you weep and pray for him. He lives as best he can. Why do you judge him? Who knows, in this world, where the sinful are?"[26] The loss of religious faith, simply through failure to practice the ritual she had learned from childhood, is another aspect of the unfolding of Guta's character.

More fortunate than either Guta or Maria José is Maria Glória, to whom destiny proves generous. In her, love comes to fruition through marriage and childbearing. The meaning of a child in the life of Guta is made clear when, as she relinquishes Maria Glória's infant, whom she had been holding, she says, "I handed her the little boy and it broke my heart. I had an absurd desire to weep, as if I were handing over all my hopes, my happiness, my consolation."[27]

Rachel's independence of thought should not be considered as aimed at the destruction of the social order or as an attack upon marriage, religion, or morals. The course followed by Noemi and by Guta is not for ordinary persons but for those few with the absolute courage of their convictions, who stand outside the bounds of society, where only grief and pain await them. As the critic Almir de Andrade has expressed it, "Rachel de Queiroz manages to reach—quietly, without emotionalism—an inner plane of life which few can boast of having been able to attain, or rather, of having been able to discover; a plane of absolute and paradoxical sincerity, which lies beyond all our conventions, all our actions motivated by hypocrisy and sham, all our prejudices and submission to routine. A plane which lies beyond good and evil."[28] Rachel de Queiroz, like her protagonists, has had the courage to invade this realm, not as an iconoclast, but as a searcher after truth. And as an artist, one of the most gifted of the present generation, she has been able to give beautiful form to her tragic but inspiring vision.

From a study of themes, characters, and social situations in Rachel's work it should be clear that a dominant characteristic is her remarkable intellect. From a girl who wrote four major novels between the ages of nineteen and twenty-eight we might hardly expect a mature fictional world, broad in its development, and rich in social and psychological content.

In view of her conciseness, the scope of the novelist's survey of society is extraordinary. Her first three novels fit easily into the three hundred fifty pages of José Olympio's recent combined edition;[29] her fourth novel is no longer than any one of these.

The unit of composition of all her novels (three of which are objectively related, the fourth, *Three Marias,* being narrated in the first person) is the short, carefully balanced chapter, often with the unity and completeness of a good short story. Rachel constructs her novels somewhat loosely, concentrating on significant moments in the lives of her characters. She avoids any pretense of a tightly woven plot. Thanks to her sense of the dramatic and her grasp of meaningful detail, monotony is rare in her novels.

The unity in the technique and construction of Rachel de Queiroz' novels is also to be found in their language. When *The Year Fifteen* was published, in 1930, the revolutionary gains made by the modernists were far from being consolidated. Therefore it is not surprising that in the preface to the first edition Rachel makes an engaging defense of the language in which the novel is written:

> When I wrote my book, I put it in the language of every day, of everybody, I let the pen flow as the tongue flows, and I arranged the verbs and the phrases, the adjectives and the pronouns (by Our Lady, the pronouns!) in our habitual workaday fashion, simply, unpretentiously, like honest country folk who put on their best Sunday-go-to-meeting clothes, but who never think of competing with the townspeople, who know what fine silk is and who wear well-tailored suits.[30]

In Brazil today it would be more appropriate, perhaps, to apologize for a literary idiom that failed to incorporate a good many elements of the popular spoken language. This has come about precisely because of the success of such books as *The Year Fifteen* and the rest of Rachel's works, which not only in the dialogue but also in the narrative remain faithful to the Portuguese spoken by Brazilians.

Colloquial speech, furthermore, provides Rachel with some of the rhythms that make her literary expression particularly effective when read aloud. We are struck by the suppleness she can impart to the Portuguese—a feminine gracefulness that never solidifies into an "arty" pose. Simplicity, sobriety, and directness are characteristic of all her writing, but are most highly refined in *Three Marias*. Rachel is fond of using figurative language, but probably does so no more often than do people in ordinary conversation. Here and there a figure of speech may have a wonderfully feminine stamp, as in this simile describing a lamp shade—"as somber and horrendous as a rain hat."[31]

Rachel's characters move always in the world of the flesh; she is concerned above all with the real world, which she paints (but does not photograph) with engaging honesty. Harsh social realities, which have been well documented by sociologists, remain harsh under her care. But her artist's hand knows when to suppress, when to add a detail, in order to achieve a desired effect.

An important aspect of Rachel's conception of the artistic duty of the novelist is absolute honesty in representing strong human emotions, particularly love, grief, and despair. Always she seems able to skirt the steep sides of a veritable canyon of sentimentality, with never a false step. That she is aware of the precipice is made clear in a statement in *Three Marias* concerning the "banality" of such revelations as Guta's suicide wish. Nevertheless, Rachel attempts to communicate profound emotion. Her control of it is one of her most admirable qualities.

Olívio Montenegro has said that the central idea in the novels of Rachel de Queiroz is the social inequality of women. He is careful to point out that she does not "ossify this idea in the form of a thesis, or glorify it as an abstraction, or pollute it in sentimental dramas."[32] The demonstration of the status and role of women in the society of the Northeast is the primary sociological merit of her books.

Rachel's chief literary merit consists in the artistic integration of the theme of women in the Northeast with the universal, timeless motif of love, spontaneous and biological, as the great imperative in the lives of all women. This daring concept of love, with its emphasis on the dignity and independence of woman, is related to a vaster idea which includes both sexes: each human being must strive to be free and must face his destiny with courage.

CHAPTER **VI**

THE NOVEL OF THE
NORTHEAST

The Novel of the Northeast

SOME THIRTY contemporary Brazilian novels have been the basis for a detailed study of four Northeastern writers. "The novel of the Northeast," a genre within a genre, has shown the utmost vitality, and future analysts of Brazilian literature must take into consideration the valuable body of writing comprehended in this generic classification. Indeed, students of Latin American literature must accord it a place alongside the Gaucho novel, the Indianist novel, the novel of the Mexican Revolution, and other important types.

A recent classification of the Brazilian novel is that of Alceu Amoroso Lima, who divides present-day writing into three categories: social, descriptive, and psychological.[1] José Lins do Rego, Jorge Amado, Rachel de Queiroz, and Graciliano Ramos are placed in the first category at the head of a list containing a few other social novelists from the Northeast and elsewhere in Brazil. In the other two categories none of the Northeasterners is to be found; this fact bears out a rather widely held notion that the Northeast (or North) produces a social literature, while the South produces one that is predominantly psychological and descriptive. This is oversimplification, of course, and results in such an anomaly as the fact that Graciliano Ramos, the social novelist, was until recently the foremost psychological novelist of Brazil. Nevertheless, Amoroso Lima's classification is useful if we remember that the social novel, or the novel of the Northeast, admits works of a good many different tendencies.

What this Brazilian critic has called "social" I have called "sociological," in referring to the nordestino novels. Because of their documentary nature they have more than literary value to students of the Brazilian scene. Sociologists give weight to the revelations of the contemporary novelists of the Northeast. An eminent American scholar, Donald Pierson, states: "They reveal in an intimate and dramatic form the character of Brazilian societies and cultures, substantially aiding our comprehension of the institutions, the relations between races, classes, and sexes, and the folkways, mores, ideas, attitudes, and sentiments, which were characteristic of Brazil at different times and places."[2] Reserving special mention for the novels of José Lins do Rego's Sugar-Cane Cycle, Professor Pierson says that they constitute, in his opinion, "indispensable reading for the understanding of the social changes which are now in process in the sugar cane regions of the Northeast."[3] Here, then, is the justification for using the term "sociological" in connection with the nordestino novel. Along with geographical settings, including flora and fauna, sociological features have been used in creating the social landscape. It has always served the ends of fiction and has existed only for the characters projected against it.

Developing some aspect of the immemorial struggle between man and his environment in the Northeast, the themes, also, have usually been sociological. José Lins do Rego's work is perhaps most notable in this respect, particularly his Sugar-Cane Cycle, along with the later *Wondrous Rock* and *Dead Fires*. Jorge Amado likewise treats the sociological theme; wherever he gazes, it is the fight for life that holds his eye. Graciliano Ramos, though individualized as a psychological novelist, must be remembered with his compatriots for showing the brutalizing and deadening effect of Northeastern geography and economics upon the man of that region. Rachel de Queiroz gives us an unusual insight into the role of woman in society.

The sociological, therefore, is no puny vein being worked to exhaustion by these novelists. The theme is substantial and embodies the writers' principal experience. All the novelists here studied were witnesses not only to the punishment of climate that sometimes singled out the Northeast for special fury but also to the process of disintegration and the upheavals in social readjustment. Thus it was inevitable that the novel of the Northeast should express the unrest of the times.

There is unquestionably much criticism of society in these novels. However, in the main the author's point of view is implied rather than stated. Rarely does the reader get the impression that he is being subjected to political propaganda. An exception must be made for Amado, almost all of whose books have urged the class struggle and class solidarity among the oppressed. *Jubiabá* is an example of the so-called proletarian literature rampant in many parts of the world in the early 'thirties. Although Ramos' last three novels appeared to be animated by a sociopolitical philosophy of revolutionary destructiveness, their meaning is too cryptic to serve as political propaganda. All the novelists treat the political theme as a consequence of their interest in reform.

The novel of the Northeast displays a new attitude toward man, a humanitarian view elaborated from the time of Euclydes da Cunha to that of Gilberto Freyre, which has contributed a distinctive quality to the contemporary novel of social content. Giving credit for this new departure to his own generation, that of the 'twenties, the critic Peregrino Júnior says: "It was the present generation that shifted the axis of Brazilian culture from 'problems of the land' to 'problems of man,' taking up the study of the Brazilian—in his history, his traditions, his customs, his language, that is, in the entirety of his 'cultural' expression—as a human, social, and economic value.'[4]

Related to the new "humanness" of the contemporary novel is the tendency to dwell upon the lives of the humble and the unfortunate. A new voice in the literature of the 'thirties is that of the nameless masses, who begin to acquire a consciousness of themselves and their role in Brazilian affairs. Modern novelists have shown themselves acutely aware that the urban and rural workers are also Brazilians and ought to be represented as human beings, not simply as statistics. Thus the shabby mestizo prisoner João Miguel gained the stature of an imposing psychological entity as presented by Rachel de Queiroz. The Negro boy Ricardo, when studied by Lins do Rego, became as dignified as his former playmate Carlos de Mello. Perhaps the most extraordinary characterization of all is Graciliano Ramos' presentation of the mental processes of the inarticulate sertanejo Fabiano in *Parched Lives*.

The effective relating of characters to the regional background is one of the important advances of contemporary Brazilian novelists over the nineteenth-century regionalists. Although they present men and women of diverse social levels, conditioned by special circumstances that are pertinent to a small corner of Brazil, their characters are nonetheless intelligible as part of all humanity. Herein lies the novelists' claim to be universal as well as regional. For example, Colonel José Paulino and his grandson Carlos de Mello, in Lins do Rego's Sugar-Cane Cycle, impress us not merely for their qualities as members of the Parahyban plantation aristocracy, but also because they are believable in terms of our own experience. The same may be said of the most engaging of Jorge Amado's characters, the lawless barons of the cacao plantations.

Of the four nordestino writers only Rachel de Queiroz, with her natural advantage, has proved able to master feminine psychology consistently in the novel. Lins do Rego is preoccupied with women, but usually they are only symbols for physical love or lust. Maria Alice and the sisters Edna and Eurídice are but shadowy incarnations of sexual passion. In all his works there is not one complete feminine character. It is a pity that Graciliano Ramos limited his explorations to the minds of his tormented male protagonists, who obviously were identified with himself. And Jorge Amado has created nothing more than momentarily intriguing and colorful feminine types, with the exception of a few heroines like Don'Ana Badaró, of *The Violent Land*.

What has been the contribution of the Northeastern writers to the form of the novel? Relatively little, it is plain. Only Graciliano Ramos as a novelist appears to have much possibility of influencing subsequent national authors in this regard. His refinement of the interior monologue and its application to contemporary Brazilian writing deserve mention. And the novel *Anguish,* because of its tiered construction of consciousness, will remain a landmark for younger writers. In novelistic conception and structure, none of the other Northeasterners has made startling departures.

Jorge Amado, José Lins do Rego, Graciliano Ramos, and Rachel de Queiroz, along with one Southerner, the short-story writer Aníbal Machado, collaborated in publishing a novel, *Brandão between His Love and the Sea (Brandão entre o Mar e o Amor).* This unusual work is of real help in comparing the differing literary styles of the four authors. It is the story of the vacillations of a Brazilian law student, Brandão, between a happy life at sea and a distasteful existence on his ancestral fazenda where he is surrounded by neurotic friends and a Brazilian-Japanese wife whom he has ceased to love. References to espionage and to Allied shipping during the Second World War must have given the work some topical interest in 1942, when it appeared. But the book is in nowise typical of the Northeastern genre. Further, it lacks coherence, and the several characters, each having five different authors, appear to have as many metamorphoses in the five chapters. Nevertheless, *Brandão* is a fascinating experiment tending to affirm the mutual exclusion implied in the terms "collective" (as applied to authorship) and "novel." But the work can afford, if not the opportunity for a detailed stylistic analysis, at least the occasion to register impressions of the salient characteristics of each novelist.

Jorge Amado begins with a long chapter setting the scene and introducing the characters, particularly Brandão's wife. Although he writes competently, he is obviously playing a part in a literary game. Absent are his lyrical enthusiasm and customary identification with his characters. There is no sociological theme, either, to elicit his partisanship, no need for linking characters to background, and nowhere any chance to give a ballad flavor to his writing. The result is flat and commonplace. Little wonder that this chapter recalls none of Amado's other work, except his boyish *Carnival Land*. Solely in a negative manner, then, does the collective novel throw any light on the style of Amado.

Like Amado, Lins do Rego, in the second chapter, seems to miss writing about regional themes and persons of significance to him. His assignment is the characterization of the book's libidinous heroine Glória, whose personal history, temperament, and neuroses are fully detailed. Glória is immediately recognizable as one of Lins do Rego's typical creatures—voluptuous, passionate, instinctive, but with few qualities other than the physical to engage the reader. The author avoids dialogue, and the entire chapter is written as a narrative soliloquy, with a seemingly artless stringing together of short, grammatically uncomplicated sentences—the oral storyteller's method which Lins do Rego has so well adapted to literature. He is perhaps most effective in conveying Glória's near-hysteria arising from her frustration and the guilt-complex stemming from her relationship with a doting father.

Graciliano Ramos' talents as a psychological novelist are revealed in the third chapter, which is a brief inward-seeking study of the tuberculous Mário, who is on the way to insanity. Mental states were the forte of the author, who describes the disease and melancholia of Mário, the cast-off husband of Glória, with a strange mixture of humor and bitterness. Humor is rare among the novelists of the Northeast; none comes closer to a smile, albeit a sardonic one, than Ramos. His pessimistic conception of mankind flavors the characterization here no less than elsewhere in his works.

The final chapter of *Brandão* is narrated by Rachel de Queiroz, who adds a note of simplicity and quietude. She has no very apparent literary manner or mannerism; her style is an extremely versatile instrument working so unobtrusively that we are all but unaware of it. Characteristically, she is observant of small details, and her synthesis of them conveys hitherto undiscovered meaning. Examples from *Brandão* are her descriptions of the hero's old town house in Bahia, and his aged mother. When she dies, Brandão dresses her in her burial garments, in a scene related with calm understanding. Death scenes are a specialty of Rachel's, and Brandão's own death brings the novel expertly to a close.

In several respects Rachel de Queiroz resembles Graciliano Ramos—"my master," as she once called him. Like Ramos, she is attracted by the sociological theme but relegates it to a secondary place, preferring to concentrate on individual psychology. The best of her works are imbued with a philosophy of personal freedom which few would dare to enunciate, but which she is able to make noble and inspiring by virtue of her art. Ramos' books are, on the contrary, animated by a harsh and bitter philosophy of life. However, though their outlooks differ, the writings of both reveal a quality of profound reflectiveness. Compared with their compatriots, Rachel and Ramos have written little, but they have written better: their writing has been more often through the purifying flames.

Lins do Rego and Jorge Amado have written voluminously and rapidly, presenting a panoramic picture of the disrupted society of the Northeast. Lins do Rego's forte has been the handling of a complex fictional world with artistry and understanding. Jorge Amado has been less successful in treating the sociological theme. Only in *The Violent Land*, where they are unadulterated by ideological considerations, do we fully perceive the imagination, enthusiasm, and lyrical feeling for reality that distinguish Amado's writing.

In contrast with Lins do Rego and Jorge Amado, Ramos makes greater use of figurative language, and his choice of adjectives is bolder and more original. Regionalisms and colloquial Brazilian expressions are frequent and are obviously chosen for their vigor, color, and appropriateness to the characters he describes. Ramos has pressed farther than any other Northeastern writer the advantage won by the vernacular over the once consecrated literary idiom of Portugal.

Paradoxically, Ramos was a polished grammarian and his refinements have led him to be fittingly described as a "purist of the vernacular."[5] Though his style is the most revolutionary in this regard, the other novelists likewise have rejected the glossy tile of Portugal in favor of the humbler brick of Brazil, and have constructed a language that reveals their own psychology and temperament. The result is a freshness of expression that is one of the truly original qualities of the new literature of Brazil.

Comparison of Ramos' literary style with that of his contemporaries illuminates his superior craftsmanship. A sense of compactness is heightened by numerous fragmentary and elliptical expressions, which, alternating with grammatically more formal writing, serve to create a striking variety of pace. For his mastery of nearly every phase of novelistic technique, and his talent for psychological exploration—a talent unmatched in Brazilian literature—Graciliano Ramos is destined to take a place alongside Machado de Assis.

Collectively, the novelists considered in this volume have demonstrated that Brazilian letters are approaching maturity.

Whether aware of it or not, they have heeded the counsel of Ronald de Carvalho, one of Brazil's most perceptive critics, concerning the best method of achieving a worthy national literature.

To create a literature of his own, the modern Brazilian should avoid any sort of prejudices. He has before his eyes a great virgin world, full of exciting promise. To organize this material, to give it stability, to reduce it to its true human dimensions and express it—these must be his fundamental concern. An art direct, pure, deeply rooted in the national foundations, an art that will affirm all our tumult as a people still in gestation—this the modern Brazilian must seek. For this, it is necessary that he study not only Brazilian problems but the great American problems as well. The primordial error of our elite up to now has been to apply artificially to Brazil the lesson of Europe. Now is the time for the lesson of America. Our time, at last, has come.[6]

Carvalho's untimely death prevented his viewing the full radiance of the literary sunburst he foretold. Among his contemporaries—novelists, essayists, poets—none seems to have better learned "the lesson of America" than Graciliano Ramos, Rachel de Queiroz, José Lins do Rego, and Jorge Amado.

These four novelists have taken a sociological theme of magnitude—a Brazilian theme that is at the same time American in its parallels and implications—and have synthesized and projected it by means of characters having both regional and universal qualities. This they have accomplished thanks to an art in which the European has been assimilated into a thoroughly Brazilian novelistic technique and idiom. Because of their achievements, the novel of the Northeast has been the outstanding literary phenomenon of Brazil in the last twenty-five years and, on a broader scale, possibly the most noteworthy artistic triumph of recent years in Latin America.

NOTES

Notes to Chapter I

INTRODUCTION

[1] Affonso Arinos de Mello Franco, *Homens e Temas do Brasil*, pp. 123–125.

[2] *Ibid.*, p. 131.

[3] See the essays of Alcides Bezerra, "Aspectos Antropográficos da Literatura Nacional," *Anuário Brasileiro de Literatura*, 1937, I, 23–26; Érico Veríssimo, *Brazilian Literature*, pp. 147–160; José Geraldo Vieira, "O Romance Brasileiro de 1930 para cá," *Boletim Bibliográfico de São Paulo*, Ano 2, IX (October–December, 1945), 33–50; Vianna Moog, *Uma Interpretação da Literatura Brasileira*.

[4] Veríssimo, *loc. cit.*

[5] Vianna Moog, *op. cit.*, pp. 15–31.

[6] Preston E. James, *Brazil*, pp. 43–44.

[7] *Ibid.*, p. 46.

[8] Gilberto Freyre, *Brazil: An Interpretation*, pp. 19–20.

[9] Gilberto Freyre, *Casa-Grande e Senzala: Formação da Família Brasileira sob o Regime de Economia Patriarcal* (4th def. ed.), trans. Samuel Putnam, *The Masters and the Slaves*.

[10] Pedro Calmon, *História da Civilização Brasileira*, p. 123.

[11] T. Lynn Smith, *Brazil: People and Institutions*, pp. 9–11.

[12] Nelson Werneck Sodré, *História da Literatura Brasileira: Seus Fundamentos Económicos* (2d ed.), p. 230.

[13] Sérgio Milliet, *Ensaios*, p. 86.

[14] Gilberto Freyre, *Nordeste*, p. 220.

[15] Euclydes da Cunha, *Os Sertões* (15th Portuguese ed.), trans. Samuel Putnam, *Rebellion in the Backlands*.

[16] *Ibid.*, translator's introduction, pp. vii–viii.

[17] Samuel Putnam has pointed out (*Marvelous Journey*, p. 204) that *Os Sertões* has recently been included in a list of one hundred of the world's best novels.

[18] *Ibid.*, p. 202.

[19] Euclydes da Cunha, *op. cit.*, p. 408.

[20] José Lins do Rego, *Poesia e Vida*, pp. 39–40.

[21] Euclydes da Cunha, *op. cit.* (English trans.), p. 85.

[22] Gilberto Freyre, *Actualidade de Euclydes da Cunha*, p. 15.

[23] Alberto Torres, *O Problema Nacional Brasileiro*. By 1938 this work had reached its third edition.

[24] Gilberto Freyre, *Região e Tradição*, p. 76.

[25] Brazilian modernism had nothing in common with Spanish American *modernismo*, the much earlier movement headed by Rubén Darío.

[26] Lawrence F. Hill, " 'Caudilhismo' versus Republicanism," in *Brazil*, p. 87.

[27] João Pandiá Calógeras, *A History of Brazil*, trans. and ed. P. A. Martin, p. 329.

[28] Jorge Amado, *Vida de Luis Carlos Prestes, el Caballero de la Esperanza*, Spanish trans. Pompeu de Accioly Borges, p. 101.

[29] *Ibid.*, p. 103.

[30] Hernane Tavares de Sá, *The Brazilians, People of Tomorrow*, p. 184.

[31] Euclydes da Cunha, *op. cit.* (English trans.), p. 153.

[32] Hill, *op. cit.*, p. 99.

[33] Amado, *op. cit.*, p. 166.

[34] *Ibid.*, p. 138.

[35] *Ibid.*, p. 242.

[36] *Ibid.*, pp. 179–180, 184.

[37] *Ibid.*, p. 32.

[38] Oswald de Andrade, *Ponta de Lança*, cited without page reference in an unsigned article, "Lembrando a Semana de Arte Moderna," *Jornal de Letras*, Ano IV, No. 32 (February, 1952), 14.

[39] Manoelito d'Ornas in *Testamento de uma Geração*, p. 177.

[40] José Pereira da Graça Aranha, *Espírito Moderno* (2d ed.), pp. 22–23.

[41] Mário de Andrade, *O Movimento Modernista*, p. 26.

[42] Putnam, *Marvelous Journey*, pp. 208–209.

[43] D. Lee Hamilton, "The *Semana de Arte Moderna* and Brazilian Modernism," *Symposium*, V (November, 1951), 190–192.

[44] This speech has been reprinted in Aranha, *op. cit.*, pp. 29–65.

[45] Also listed as *Cancioneiro de Oswald de Andrade*.

[46] Hamilton, *op. cit.*, p. 189.

[47] *Ibid.*

[48] José Cândido de Andrade Muricy, *A Nova Literatura Brasileira*, pp. 353–354.

[49] *Ibid.*, p. 354.

[50] João Alphonsus in *Testamento de uma Geração*, p. 156.

[51] José Osório de Oliveira, *História Breve da Literatura Brasileira* (new ed. rev.), p. 127.

[52] Freyre, *Região e Tradição*, preface by Lins do Rego, p. 11.

[53] Freyre, *Perfil de Euclydes e Outros Perfis*, pp. 175–181. An enduring contribution to *Livro do Nordeste* is the treasured "Evocação do Recife" by Manuel Bandeira, a poem that would never have been written without Gilberto's insistence.

[54] Freyre, *Brazil: An Interpretation*, p. 177.

[55] Freyre, *Casa-Grande e Senzala* (1st ed.), preface, reprinted in *The Masters and the Slaves*, pp. xx–xxi.

[56] *Ibid.*

[57] José António Gonçalves de Mello, *No Tempo dos Flamengos*, p. 34.

[58] *Ibid.*

[59] Mello Franco, *op. cit.*, p. 84.

[60] Freyre, *Brazil: An Interpretation*, p. 176.

[61] Freyre, *Região e Tradição*, p. 26.

[62] Freyre, *Brazil: An Interpretation*, p. 179.

[63] Freyre refrains from including in his immediate group, with Recife as its center, other novelists such as Amando Fontes, Rachel de Queiroz, Graciliano Ramos, and Jorge Amado, all from other areas of the Northeast.

[64] José Américo de Almeida, *A Parahyba e Seus Problemas*.

[65] *Ibid.*, p. 472.

[66] Prudente de Morais Neto, *The Brazilian Romance*, trans. Luis Víctor le Cocq d'Oliveira, pp. 34–36.

[67] H. de Lima and G. Barroso, *Pequeno Dicionário Brasileiro da Língua Portuguesa* (7th ed.).

[68] José Américo de Almeida, *A Bagaceira* (6th ed.), pp. 8–9.

[69] Andrade Muricy, *op. cit.*, p. 311.

[70] José Américo de Almeida, *A Bagaceira*, p. 286.

[71] Alphonsus, *op. cit.*, p. 147. Américo was enthusiastic about modernism, but probably no more so than was Freyre himself when he discovered that some of the modernists had interests in Brazilian life and culture paralleling his own.

[72] Amado, *op. cit.*, p. 235.

[73] Harvey Walker, "The Vargas Regime," in *Brazil*, pp. 108–109.

[74] José Simplício, *Retrato Popular de um Homem*, p. 68.

[75] More than 70,000 federal troops were ranged against 28,000 revolutionists. P. A. Martin, "The Last Decade of Brazilian History," appended to Calógeras, *A History of Brazil*, p. 342.

[76] Amado, *op. cit.*, p. 233.

[77] *Ibid.*, pp. 268–269.

[78] *Ibid.*, p. 270.

[79] *Ibid.*, p. 272.

[80] Walker, *op. cit.*, p. 113.

[81] Amado, *op. cit.*, p. 274.

[82] P. A. Martin, in Calógeras, *A History of Brazil*, p. 346.

[83] Amado, *op. cit.*, p. 301.

[84] Almir de Andrade, *Aspectos da Cultura Brasileira*, p. 7.

[85] Lia Correa Dutra, *O Romance Brasileiro e José Lins do Rego*, p. 10.

[86] Sérgio Milliet, *Diário Crítico*, III, 71.

[87] Olívio Montenegro, *O Romance Brasileiro*, p. 24.

[88] José Benedicto Silveira Peixoto, *Falam os Escritores*, II, 145.

[89] Milliet, *Ensaios*, pp. 185–186.

[90] Peregrino Júnior, "Sobre Alguns Livros," *Lanterna Verde*, No. 1 (May, 1934), 57.

[91] Milliet, *Diário Crítico*, I, 299.

[92] Diogo de Mello Menezes, *Gilberto Freyre*, p. 198.

[93] Freyre, *The Masters and the Slaves*, "In Lieu of a Preface to the Third Edition," p. lxii.

[94] Amado, *op. cit.*, p. 293. See also Ralph E. Dimmick, "The Brazilian Literary Generation of 1930," *Hispania*, XXXIV (May, 1951), 184.

[95] Walker, *op. cit.*, p. 114.

[96] *Ibid.*

[97] Departamento de Imprensa e Propaganda, "Os Maus Livros," *O Brasil de Hoje, de Ontem e de Amanhã*, Vol. I, No. 9 (September 30, 1940), 25–26.

[98] Departamento de Imprensa e Propaganda, "A Literatura Dissolvente," *ibid.*, No. 2 (February 29, 1940), 23–24.

[99] Departamento de Imprensa e Propaganda, *Brasil dos Nossos Dias.* See the articles "O Culto do Passado," pp. 13–17; "O Estado e a Cultura," pp. 19–21; and "A Arte do Regime," pp. 69–73.

[100] Mello Menezes, *op. cit.*, pp. 197–199.

[101] Samuel Putnam, "Brazilian Culture under Vargas," *Science and Society*, VI (Winter, 1942), 51.

[102] All four contributed, however, to a collective novel, *Brandão entre o Mar e o Amor.* This literary experiment is further discussed in chapter vi.

[103] The attitude of Lins do Rego with respect to the dictatorship of Vargas is somewhat equivocal. If it is true, as has been stated, that he led a "loyalty embassy" to Vargas, his statements made outside Brazil and published in his *Conferências no Prata* (1946) show him nevertheless to be a staunch advocate of liberal democracy and, like his compatriots, an enemy of authoritarian government. The lectures included in this work were delivered in October, 1943. The date of publication is significant. His views on dictators and freedom of thought are expressed in the preface to the lectures.

[104] Samuel Putnam, "Brazilian Literature," *Handbook of Latin American Studies, 1936*, II, 337.

[105] Putnam, "The Brazilian Social Novel," *Inter-American Quarterly*, II (April, 1940), 10.

[106] Putnam, "Brazilian Culture under Vargas," *Science and Society*, VI (Winter, 1942), 43.

[107] *Ibid.*, p. 49.

[108] The posthumous *Memórias do Cárcere* (4 vols.; Rio de Janeiro, 1953), dealing autobiographically with the period of Ramos' imprisonment, was not available for inclusion in the present study.

[109] Unsigned article, "Alguns Lançamentos de 1952," *Jornal de Letras*, Ano IV (January, 1952), 9. Rachel de Queiroz has also recently published a noteworthy play, *Lampião, Drama em Cinco Quadros* (Rio de Janeiro, 1953), with a theme of banditry in the Northeast.

[110] Putnam, "The Brazilian Social Novel," *Inter-American Quarterly*, II (April, 1940), 11.

[111] José Lins do Rego, *Cangaceiros* (Rio de Janeiro, 1953). I have not yet seen this novel, which is heralded as one of his greatest.

[112] António Callado, "A Literary Letter from Brazil," *New York Times Book Review*, June 10, 1951, p. 29.

Notes to Chapter II

JOSÉ LINS DO REGO

[1] Nelson Werneck Sodré, *Orientações do Pensamento Brasileiro*, p. 125.

[2] In the manner of Kentucky, certain Brazilian states have granted patents or commissions of high military rank in the state militia to men of social and political importance. In the novels of Amado, *coronéis* (colonels) are often synony-

mous with the class of landholders and planters along the agricultural seaboard and elsewhere.

[3] Sodré, *op. cit.*, p. 127.

[4] Olívio Montenegro, *O Romance Brasileiro*, pp. 131–132.

[5] Sodré, *op. cit.*, p. 132.

[6] Gilberto Freyre, *Região e Tradição*, preface, p. 9.

[7] On Lins do Rego's attitude toward modernism, see the essay "Jorge de Lima e o Modernismo," dated 1926, reprinted in his *Gordos e Magros*, pp. 6–32.

[8] Freyre, *op. cit.*, preface, p. 21.

[9] *Gordos e Magros*, author's preface, p. xii.

[10] *Ibid.*, p. xiii.

[11] See Lins do Rego's essay of 1935 (written in conjunction with Gilberto Freyre), "No Brasil também se Morre de Fome," and also one of the year 1941, "E João Rouco," reprinted in *Gordos e Magros*, pp. 266–270, and 209–212, respectively.

[12] José Osório de Morais Borba, *A Comédia Literária*, pp. 230–231.

[13] Sérgio Milliet, *Diário Crítico*, I, 299–300.

[14] *Usina*, author's introduction, p. 7.

[15] Gilberto Freyre, *The Masters and the Slaves*, p. 399.

[16] *Banguê*, p. 9.

[17] *Menino de Engenho*, pp. 137–138.

[18] *Ibid.*, p. 131.

[19] *Banguê*, p. 18.

[20] Jayme de Barros, *Espelho dos Livros*, I, 109.

[21] Montenegro, *op. cit.*, pp. 142–143.

[22] *Menino de Engenho*, p. 159.

[23] Roberto Alvim Correa, *Anteu e a Crítica*, p. 158.

[24] In his *A Língua do Nordeste* (2d ed.), p. 21, the linguist Mário Marroquim has called *Menino de Engenho* "a literary document of dialectology."

[25] *O Moleque Ricardo*, pp. 15–16.

[26] *Ibid.*, p. 250.

[27] Once, when asked to name the masters who had influenced his literary style, Lins do Rego replied, "the blind street singers at the fairs of Parahyba and Pernambuco," adding, "When I imagine my novels, I always take as my guiding plan of orientation the writing of things as they come to my memory, in the simple form and manner of the blind poets . . ." *Poesia e Vida*, pp. 54–55. Elsewhere the novelist describes his impressions of the prose and verse tales heard from old Totónia, the Negress who used to come to the plantations to regale the children with stories. *Gordos e Magros*, p. 278.

[28] *Menino de Engenho* (3d ed.), introductory note by Prudente de Morais Neto [pseud. Pedro Dantas], pp. xii–xiii.

[29] Barros, *op. cit.*, p. 109.

[30] According to Sodré, *op. cit.*, p. 139, the short novel *Pureza* was written in less than a month.

[31] Almir de Andrade, *Aspectos da Cultura Brasileira*, p. 134.

[32] *Pureza*, p. 82.

[33] Euclydes da Cunha, *Os Sertões* (15th Portuguese ed.), pp. 143–144.

[34] José Osório de Oliveira, *História Breve da Literatura Brasileira* (new ed. rev.), p. 148.

[35] In *Riacho Doce,* in a chapter describing Carlos' moral breakdown, we read: "there only alcohol would give him strength for that existence . . . and whiskey kept giving him strength for his weaknesses" (p. 305); "and the peace that whiskey gave him was the only peace that existed . . . but whiskey had kept him going until the next day" (p. 307); "it [whiskey] was the only thing that could bind him to life . . . only whiskey gave him the courage to stand up against such misery" (p. 308); "whiskey alone would have the capacity to maintain him there without his becoming desperate . . . only whiskey could give him the courage to flee his weaknesses" (p. 309); "but whiskey was good for everything" (p. 312).

[36] Freyre, *The Masters and the Slaves,* pp. 138–139.

[37] Sodré, *op. cit.,* p. 135.

[38] *Poesia e Vida,* p. 54.

[39] Álvaro Lins, "Um Novo Romance dos Engenhos," *Correio da Manhã,* February 4, 1944, reprinted in *Fogo Morto* (2d ed.), p. 366.

[40] *Fogo Morto* (2d ed.), p. 339.

[41] *Eurídice* (3d ed.), p. 42.

[42] *Ibid.,* p. 117.

[43] *Ibid.,* p. 154.

[44] *Ibid.,* p. 244.

[45] *Ibid.,* p. 192.

[46] *Fogo Morto,* preface, p. 11.

[47] Álvaro Lins, *op. cit.,* pp. 369–370.

Notes to Chapter III

JORGE AMADO

[1] Nelson Werneck Sodré, *Orientações do Pensamento Brasileiro,* p. 156. He also notes that about 1932 Amado wrote a novel, hitherto unpublished, entitled *O Ruy Barbosa No. 2* describing life at this school, which was located in a former residence of the poet Castro Alves, in whom the novelist later became greatly interested. *Orientações,* p. 162.

[2] *Bahia de Todos os Santos: Guia das Ruas e dos Mistérios da Cidade do Salvador,* p. 50.

[3] Sodré, *op. cit.,* p. 160.

[4] *O País do Carnaval* (4th ed.), bound in one volume with *Cacáu* (4th ed.), and *Suor* (3d ed.).

[5] *Capitães da Areia,* preface, p. 12.

[6] Álvaro Lins, *Jornal de Crítica,* V, 138.

[7] *O País do Carnaval,* p. 114.

[8] *Ibid.,* pp. 11–12.

[9] Álvaro Lins, *op. cit.,* V, 135–136.

[10] The publisher, Livraria Martins Editôra, states that *Cacáu* has been translated into Russian and Spanish. It first appeared in 1933.

[11] *Ibid.* (4th ed.), p. 204.

[12] *Terras do Sem Fim* (3d ed.), trans. Samuel Putnam, *The Violent Land.*

[13] *Capitães da Areia,* preface, p. 16.

[14] *Terras do Sem Fim* (3d Portuguese ed.), p. 45.

[15] *Ibid.*, p. 56.
[16] *Ibid.*, p. 274.
[17] Preston E. James, *Brazil*, pp. 62–64.
[18] Donald Pierson, *Negroes in Brazil*, p. 20.
[19] *Ibid.*, p. 222.
[20] First published in 1934, *Suor*, according to the publisher, has been translated into English, Spanish, Yiddish, and Russian.
[21] *Bahia de Todos os Santos*, p. 98. See Gilberto Freyre, *Sobrados e Mucambos*, for a discussion of the role of these mansions of the wealthy rural aristocracy in the social life of the eighteenth and nineteenth centuries.
[22] First published in 1935, *Jubiabá* has been translated into French, Russian, English, German, Swedish, Danish, and Spanish, and also adapted for theater and radio, according to publisher's information.
[23] Sodré, *op. cit.*, p. 163.
[24] Artur Ramos, *The Negro in Brazil*, p. 150.
[25] *Jubiabá* (3d ed.), p. 18.
[26] *Ibid.*, p. 266.
[27] Gilberto Freyre, *Brazil: An Interpretation*, p. 158.
[28] Ramos, *op. cit.*, pp. 149–150.
[29] *Jubiabá*, p. 95.
[30] *Ibid.*, p. 305.
[31] Winner of the Graça Aranha prize for the best novel of 1936, *Mar Morto* has been translated into English, French, and Spanish, and has been adapted for motion picture and radio.
[32] *Ibid.* (2d ed.), p. 26.
[33] Pierson, *op. cit.*, p. 254.
[34] *Mar Morto*, pp. 267–268.
[35] *Capitães da Areia* has been translated into Spanish.
[36] *Ibid.*, p. 38.
[37] *Ibid.*, p. 143.
[38] *Ibid.*, p. 343.
[39] José Cândido de Andrade Muricy, *A Nova Literatura Brasileira*, p. 299.
[40] *Who's Who in Latin America* (3d ed.), Part VI, *Brazil*, p. 10.
[41] *Seara Vermelha*, p. 228.
[42] Sérgio Milliet, *Diário Crítico*, IV, 148.
[43] *São Jorge dos Ilhéus* (2d ed.), p. 9.
[44] See *ibid.*, pp. 240–249, for the curious scene in which Joaquim, following what he states to be Communist dogma, reproves the poet Sérgio Moura and his paramour Julieta for their illicit relationship.
[45] *Capitães da Areia*, p. 203.
[46] Amado's attitude toward the fazendeiro is expressed in *Cacáu*, p. 172; *São Jorge dos Ilhéus*, p. 138; *Seara Vermelha*, p. 56. Regarding the overseer: "Everyone hates the overseer more than the Colonel. The Colonel is untouchable, he is sacred, but the overseer was himself once a worker, he is equal to everyone, except that he has improved himself, and now he is worse than the boss himself." *São Jorge dos Ilhéus*, p. 108. See also *Jubiabá*, p. 164; *Cacáu*, p. 172. Amado's attitude toward the clergy is expressed in *Suor*, p. 251, and in the figures of Father Clovis and the Canon of *Capitães da Areia*, pp. 99 and 198, respectively. A notable exception is Father José Pedro of the latter novel. A strikebreaker is pictured in *Capitães da*

Areia, p. 336; an American businessman, in *Jubiabá*, p. 280, and in *São Jorge dos Ilhéus*, p. 305. Mention of the motion picture is in *Suor*, p. 281.

[47] *Capitães da Areia*, p. 315.

[48] *Vida de Luis Carlos Prestes*, p. 157.

[49] *Suor*, pp. 256, 313–314; *Jubiabá*, pp. 305–306; *Capitães da Areia*, pp. 169, 300; *Cacáu*, pp. 196, 204; *São Jorge dos Ilhéus*, pp. 59, 70; *Seara Vermelha*, pp. 255, 306.

[50] Olívio Montenegro, *O Romance Brasileiro*, p. 149.

[51] *Ibid.*, p. 145.

[52] "They were the sounds of drum beats descending from all the hills, sounds which on the other side of the ocean had been warlike sounds, drum beats which resounded to announce combats or hunts. Today they were the sounds of supplication, enslaved voices asking for help, legions of Negroes with hands outstretched to heaven. Some of those black men, their woolly heads now white, still had the lash-marks on their backs. Today the macumbas and the candomblés were sending down those long-lost sounds." *Jubiabá*, p. 120.

[53] *Mar Morto*, p. 15.

[54] "A poem of action, a true *geste*," as Câmara Cascudo has called it, the *ABC* is a form of folk ballad found especially in the North and Northeast. Its verse has seven syllables (according to the Portuguese or French count), and it takes its name from the mnemonic device whereby each four-line or six-line strophe begins with a different letter of the alphabet. Its heroes are taken from sertanejo life; its subject matter may include love stories, criminal escapades, tales of animals, or scenes of rural life. Luis da Câmara Cascudo, *Vaqueiros e Cantadores*, pp. 53–63.

[55] Milliet, *Diário Crítico*, I, 227. The translation is from *Terras do Sem Fim* (3d ed.), p. 139: "Once upon a time there were three sisters who were alike in their youthful escapades and in their hearty laughter. Lúcia of the black braids; Violeta of the lusterless eyes; Maria the youngest of the three. Once upon a time there were three sisters who were alike in the fate that befell them."

[56] Montenegro, *op. cit.*, p. 150.

[57] Álvaro Lins, *op. cit.*, p. 133.

Notes to Chapter IV

GRACILIANO RAMOS

[1] Ralph E. Dimmick, "The Brazilian Literary Generation of 1930," *Hispania*, XXXIV (May, 1951), 182.

[2] Compare *Infância*, p. 23, and *Angústia* (2d ed.), pp. 34–35.

[3] *Infância*, p. 252.

[4] *Ibid.*, p. 258.

[5] Nelson Werneck Sodré, *Orientações do Pensamento Brasileiro*, p. 107.

[6] José Osório de Morais Borba, *A Comédia Literária*, p. 236.

[7] *Infância*, pp. 232–233.

[8] "Os Romancistas Falam de Seus Personagens—Paulo Honório de *São Bernardo*," *Jornal de Letras*, Ano I, No. 6 (December, 1949), 2.

[9] Osório Borba, *op. cit.*, p. 235.

[10] José Lins do Rego, *Poesia e Vida*, p. 247.

[11] Osório Borba, *op. cit.*, p. 238.

[12] H. Pereira da Silva, *Graciliano Ramos: Ensaio Crítico Psicanalítico*, p. 96.

[13] *Ibid.*, p. 63.

[14] *Who's Who in Latin America* (3d ed.), Part VI, *Brazil*, p. 209, lists for Ramos, under membership, "Partido Comunista do Brasil."

[15] "Graciliano Ramos e o Romance: Ensaio de Interpretação," introductory essay by Floriano Gonçalves, in *Caetés*, pp. 29–30.

[16] Otto Maria Carpeaux, *Origens e Fins*, pp. 346–347.

[17] *Ibid.*, pp. 348–350.

[18] Álvaro Lins, *Jornal de Crítica*, II, 82.

[19] Osório Borba, *op. cit.*, pp. 239–240.

[20] Almir de Andrade, *Aspectos da Cultura Brasileira*, p. 97.

[21] *Caetés* (2d ed.), p. 139.

[22] *Ibid.*, p. 216.

[23] *Ibid.*, pp. 215–216.

[24] *Ibid.*, p. 166.

[25] Introductory essay by Gonçalves, in *Caetés*, p. 37.

[26] *Caetés*, p. 100. It is not surprising that "tibicoara" is not registered in H. de Lima and G. Barroso, *Pequeno Dicionário Brasileiro* (7th ed.).

[27] *Caetés*, p. 161.

[28] *São Bernardo* (2d ed.), pp. 248–249.

[29] *Ibid.*, p. 251.

[30] *Ibid.*, p. 253.

[31] *Ibid.*, p. 254.

[32] *Ibid.*, pp. 212–213.

[33] *Ibid.*, pp. 9–10.

[34] *Ibid.*, p. 13.

[35] *Angústia*, p. 198.

[36] *Ibid.*

[37] Álvaro Lins, *Jornal de Crítica*, II, 78.

[38] *Vidas Secas*, p. 25.

[39] *Ibid.*, pp. 145–146.

[40] *Ibid.*, p. 197.

[41] Pereira da Silva, *op. cit.*, p. 119.

[42] See those published in Ramos, *Histórias Incompletas*. Short-story collections are *Histórias de Alexandre, Dois Dedos*, and *Insônia*. According to advance reports, his posthumous autobiographical *Memórias do Cárcere* is also narrated in short-story form.

[43] Osório Borba, *op. cit.*, p. 242.

[44] Guilherme de Figueiredo, "Alguns Romances de '38," *Anuário Brasileiro de Literatura, 1939*, III, 73.

[45] "Os Romancistas Falam," *Jornal de Letras*, Ano I, No. 6 (December, 1949), 2.

Notes to Chapter V

RACHEL DE QUEIROZ

[1] Unsigned article, "Perfil de Rachel de Queiroz," *Folha da Manhã*, April 9, 1950, Sunday supplement.

[2] *A Donzela e a Moura Torta: Crónicas e Reminiscências*, pp. 200–201.

[3] *Ibid.*, p. 161.

[4] *O Quinze* (4th ed. rev.), issued with *João Miguel* (2d ed. rev.) and *Caminho de Pedras* (2d ed. rev.) in a single volume, *Três Romances*.

[5] Alceu Amoroso Lima [pseud. Tristão de Athayde], *Estudos*, V, 93.

[6] *O Quinze*, pp. 58–59.

[7] António Cândido, "The Brazilian Family," in *Brazil: Portrait of Half a Continent*, p. 308.

[8] *O Quinze*, p. 51.

[9] *Ibid.*, p. 120.

[10] See note 4, above.

[11] An excellent summary of the social causes of prostitution in Brazil is given by António Cândido: "A widely accepted idea is that the boy needs to *desemburrar*—that is, to begin his sexual life precociously. Hence the tolerance for prostitution, which may be said to be an indispensable complement of the present familial organization in Brazil: if girls retain their virginity, if marriage is indissoluble, if boys commence their sex life early, and if husbands have a certain right to infidelity, clearly there must be a certain class of women to equilibrate the situation. And, as in other countries, the ranks of the prostitutes are filled with girls from among the common people, whose financial difficulties or the loss of virginity lead them to seek this means of livelihood." *Op. cit.*, p. 310.

[12] *João Miguel*, p. 222.

[13] *Ibid.*, p. 150.

[14] *Ibid.*, p. 213.

[15] *Ibid.*, p. 231.

[16] *Ibid.*, p. 234.

[17] See note 4, above.

[18] Almir de Andrade, "Caminho de Pedras," *Boletim de Ariel*, Ano VI, No. 9 (June, 1937), 274.

[19] *Ibid.*, p. 275.

[20] *Caminho de Pedras*, p. 276.

[21] *Ibid.*, p. 304.

[22] *Ibid.*, pp. 341–342.

[23] *Ibid.*, p. 349.

[24] *As Três Marias* (2d ed.), p. 26.

[25] *Ibid.*, p. 157.

[26] *Ibid.*, pp. 271–272.

[27] *Ibid.*, p. 277.

[28] Almir de Andrade, *loc. cit.*

[29] See note 4, above.

[30] Reprinted in *O Quinze* (2d ed.), p. 6.

[31] *As Três Marias*, p. 229.
[32] Olívio Montenegro, *O Romance Brasileiro*, p. 176.

Notes to Chapter VI

THE NOVEL OF THE NORTHEAST

[1] Alceu Amoroso Lima, "O Romance Modernista," mimeographed copy of an address circulated at the Portuguese section of the Modern Language Association meeting at Boston, Massachusetts, December 27, 1952.

[2] Donald Pierson, "Sociologia," in *Manual Bibliográfico de Estudos Brasileiros*, p. 796.

[3] *Ibid.*

[4] Peregrino Júnior, in *Testamento de uma Geração*, p. 217.

[5] H. Pereira da Silva, *Graciliano Ramos: Ensaio Crítico Psicanalítico*, p. 16.

[6] Ronald de Carvalho, *Pequena História da Literatura Brasileira* (6th ed.), p. 372.

BIBLIOGRAPHY

Bibliography

NOVELS OF THE FOUR MASTERS

Brandão entre o Mar e o Amor. São Paulo, Livraria Martins, 1942.

JOSÉ LINS DO REGO

Agua-Mãe. 2d ed.; Rio de Janeiro, José Olympio, 1942.
Banguê. Rio de Janeiro, José Olympio, 1934.
Cangaceiros. Rio de Janeiro, José Olympio, 1953.
Doidinho. 2d ed.; Rio de Janeiro, José Olympio, 1935.
Eurídice. 3d ed.; Rio de Janeiro, José Olympio, 1948.
Fogo Morto. 2d ed.; Rio de Janeiro, José Olympio, 1944.
Menino de Engenho. 3d ed.; Rio de Janeiro, José Olympio, 1939.
O Moleque Ricardo. 2d ed.; Rio de Janeiro, José Olympio, 1936.
Pedra Bonita. 2d ed.; Rio de Janeiro, José Olympio, 1939.
Pureza. Rio de Janeiro, José Olympio, 1937.
Riacho Doce. Rio de Janeiro, José Olympio, 1939.
Usina. Rio de Janeiro, José Olympio, 1936.

JORGE AMADO

Cacáu. 4th ed.; São Paulo, Livraria Martins, 1944.
Capitães da Areia. Rio de Janeiro, José Olympio, 1937.
Jubiabá. 3d ed.; São Paulo, Livraria Martins, 1944.
Mar Morto. 2d ed.; São Paulo, Livraria Martins, 1942.
O País do Carnaval. 4th ed.; São Paulo, Livraria Martins, 1944.
São Jorge dos Ilhéus. 2d ed.; São Paulo, Livraria Martins, 1944.
Seara Vermelha. São Paulo, Livraria Martins, 1946.
Suor. 3d ed.; São Paulo, Livraria Martins, 1944.
Terras do Sem Fim. 3d ed.; São Paulo, Livraria Martins, 1944.

GRACILIANO RAMOS

Angústia. 2d ed.; Rio de Janeiro, José Olympio, 1941.
Caetés. 2d ed.; Rio de Janeiro, José Olympio, 1947.

184 BIBLIOGRAPHY

Dois Dedos. Rio de Janeiro, José Olympio, 1945. A collection of short stories.
Histórias de Alexandre. Rio de Janeiro, Companhia Editôra Leitura, 1944. A collection of short stories.
Histórias Incompletas. Pôrto Alegre, Livraria do Globo, 1946. A collection of short stories.
Insônia. Rio de Janeiro, José Olympio, 1947. A collection of short stories.
São Bernardo. 2d ed.; Rio de Janeiro, José Olympio, 1938.
Vidas Secas. Rio de Janeiro, José Olympio, 1938.

RACHEL DE QUEIROZ

As Três Marias. 2d ed.; Rio de Janeiro, José Olympio, 1943.
Três Romances. Rio de Janeiro, José Olympio, 1948. Includes the three novels *Caminho de Pedras* (2d ed.), *João Miguel* (2d ed.), and *O Quinze* (4th ed.).

LITERATURE CITED

Alvim Correa, Roberto. *Anteu e a Crítica.* Rio de Janeiro, José Olympio, 1948.
Amado, Jorge. *Bahia de Todos os Santos: Guia das Ruas e dos Mistérios da Cidade do Salvador.* São Paulo, Livraria Martins, 1945.
———. *Vida de Luis Carlos Prestes, el Caballero de la Esperanza.* Spanish translation by Pompeu de Accioly Borges. Buenos Aires, Editorial Claridad, 1942.
Américo de Almeida, José. *A Bagaceira.* 6th ed.; Rio de Janeiro, José Olympio, 1936.
———. *A Parahyba e Seus Problemas.* Parahyba, Imprensa Oficial, 1924.
Amoroso Lima, Alceu [pseud. Tristão de Athayde]. *Estudos.* Rio de Janeiro, Civilização Brasileira, 1933.
Andrade, Almir de. *Aspectos da Cultura Brasileira.* Rio de Janeiro, Schmidt Editôra, 1939.
Andrade, Mário de. *Macunaíma: O Herói sem Nenhum Carácter.* 2d ed.; Rio de Janeiro, José Olympio, 1937.
———. *Paulicéia Desvairada.* São Paulo, Casa Mayença, 1922.
———. *O Movimento Modernista.* Rio de Janeiro, Casa do Estudante do Brasil, 1942.
Andrade, Oswald de. *Pau Brasil.* Paris, "Sans Pareil," 1925.
Andrade Muricy, José Cândido de. *A Nova Literatura Brasileira: Crítica e Antologia.* Pôrto Alegre, Livraria do Globo, 1936.
Barros, Jayme de. *Espelho dos Livros.* Rio de Janeiro, José Olympio, 1936.
Bezerra, Alcides. "Aspectos Antropográficos da Literatura Nacional," *Anuário Brasileiro de Literatura, 1937.* Rio de Janeiro, Irmãos Pongetti, 1937.
Borba de Moraes, Rubens, and William Berrien, eds. *Manual Bibliográfico de Estudos Brasileiros.* Rio de Janeiro, Gráfica Editôra Souza, 1949.
Brazil. Departamento de Imprensa e Propaganda. *Brasil dos Nossos Dias.* Rio de Janeiro, 1940.
Calmon, Pedro. *História da Civilização Brasileira.* São Paulo, Companhia Editôra Nacional, 1933.
Calógeras, João Pandiá. *A History of Brazil.* Translated and edited by P. A. Martin, Chapel Hill, University of North Carolina Press, 1939.
Câmara Cascudo, Luis da. *Vaqueiros e Cantadores.* Pôrto Alegre, Livraria do Globo, 1939.

Cândido, António. "The Brazilian Family," in *Brazil: Portrait of Half a Continent*, edited by T. Lynn Smith and Alexander Marchant. New York, The Dryden Press, Inc., 1951.

Carpeaux, Otto Maria. *Origens e Fins*. Rio de Janeiro, Casa do Estudante do Brasil, 1943.

Carvalho, Ronald de. *Pequena História da Literatura Brasileira*. 6th ed.; Rio de Janeiro, F. Briguiet e Cia., 1937.

Cavalheiro, Edgard, ed. *Testamento de uma Geração*. Pôrto Alegre, Livraria do Globo, 1944.

Correa Dutra, Lia. *O Romance Brasileiro e José Lins do Rego*. Lisbon, Cadernos da "Seara Nova," 1938.

Cunha, Euclydes da. *Os Sertões*. 15th ed.; Rio de Janeiro, Livraria Francisco Alves, 1940. Translated as *Rebellion in the Backlands*, by Samuel Putnam. Chicago, University of Chicago Press, 1944.

Figueiredo, Guilherme de. "Alguns Romances de '38," *Anuário Brasileiro de Literatura, 1939*. Rio de Janeiro, Irmãos Pongetti, 1939.

Freyre, Gilberto. *Actualidade de Euclydes da Cunha*. Rio de Janeiro, Casa do Estudante do Brasil, 1941.

———. *Brazil: An Interpretation*. New York, Alfred A. Knopf, Inc., 1945.

———. *Casa-Grande e Senzala: Formação da Família Brasileira sob o Regime de Economia Patriarcal*. 4th def. ed.; Rio de Janeiro, José Olympio, 1943. 2 vols. Translated as *The Masters and the Slaves*, by Samuel Putnam. New York, Alfred A. Knopf, Inc., 1946.

———. *Nordeste*. Rio de Janeiro, José Olympio, 1937.

———. *Perfil de Euclydes e Outros Perfis*. Rio de Janeiro, José Olympio, 1944.

———. *Região e Tradição*. Rio de Janeiro, José Olympio, 1941.

———. *Sobrados e Mucambos*. São Paulo, Companhia Editôra Nacional, 1936.

Gonçalves, Floriano. "Graciliano Ramos e o Romance: Ensaio de Interpretação," in *Caetés*. 2d ed.; Rio de Janeiro, José Olympio, 1947.

Gonçalves de Mello, José António. *No Tempo dos Flamengos*. Rio de Janeiro, José Olympio, 1947.

Graça Aranha, José Pereira da. *Espírito Moderno*. 2d ed.; São Paulo, Companhia Editôra Nacional, 1932.

Hanke, Lewis, ed. *Handbook of Latin American Studies, 1936*. Cambridge, Mass.; Harvard University Press, 1937.

Hill, Lawrence F. " 'Caudilhismo' versus Republicanism," in *Brazil*, edited by Lawrence F. Hill. Berkeley and Los Angeles, University of California Press, 1947.

Hilton, Ronald, ed. *Who's Who in Latin America*. Part VI, Brazil. 3d. ed.; Stanford, Calif., Stanford University Press, 1948.

James, Preston E. *Brazil*. New York, The Odyssey Press, Inc., 1946.

Lins, Álvaro. *Jornal de Crítica*. Rio de Janeiro, José Olympio, 1947.

Lins do Rego, José. *Conferências no Prata*. Rio de Janeiro, Casa do Estudante do Brasil, 1946.

———. "E João Rouco," in *Gordos e Magros*. Rio de Janeiro, Casa do Estudante do Brasil, 1942.

———. "Jorge de Lima e o Modernismo," in *Gordos e Magros*.

———. *Poesia e Vida*. Rio de Janeiro, Editôra Universal, 1945.

Lins do Rego, José, and Gilberto Freyre. "No Brasil também se Morre de Fome," in *Gordos e Magros.*

Marroquim, Mário. *A Língua do Nordeste.* 2d ed.; São Paulo, Companhia Editôra Nacional, 1945.

Mello Franco, Affonso Arinos de. *Homens e Temas do Brasil.* Rio de Janeiro, Valverde Editôra, 1944.

Mello Menezes, Diogo de. *Gilberto Freyre.* Rio de Janeiro, Casa do Estudante do Brasil, 1944.

Milliet, Sérgio. *Diário Crítico.* São Paulo, Editôra Brasiliense, 1944; São Paulo, Livraria Martins, 1945.

———. *Ensaios.* São Paulo, Sociedade Impressora Brasileira, Brusco e Cia., 1938.

Montenegro, Olívio. *O Romance Brasileiro.* Rio de Janeiro, José Olympio, 1938.

Morais Neto, Prudente de. *The Brazilian Romance.* Translated by Luis Víctor le Cocq d'Oliveira. Rio de Janeiro, Ministry of State for Foreign Affairs of Brazil, Division of Intellectual Coöperation, Imprensa Nacional, 1943.

Osório de Morais Borba, José. *A Comédia Literária.* Rio de Janeiro, Alba Editôra, 1941.

Osório de Oliveira, José. *História Breve da Literatura Brasileira.* Rev. ed.; São Paulo, Livraria Martins, 1946.

Pereira da Silva, H. *Graciliano Ramos: Ensaio Crítico Psicanalítico.* Rio de Janeiro, Editôra Aurora Limitada, 1950.

Pierson, Donald. *Negroes in Brazil.* Chicago, University of Chicago Press, 1942.

Putnam, Samuel. "Brazilian Literature," in *Handbook of Latin American Studies, 1936.* Cambridge, Mass., Harvard University Press, 1937.

———. *Marvelous Journey.* New York, Alfred A. Knopf, Inc., 1948.

Queiroz, Rachel de. *A Donzela e a Moura Torta: Crónicas e Reminiscências.* Rio de Janeiro, José Olympio, 1948.

Ramos, Artur. *The Negro in Brazil.* Translated by Richard Pattee. Washington, D.C., The Associated Publishers, Inc., 1939.

Ramos, Graciliano. *Infância.* Rio de Janeiro, José Olympio, 1945.

———. *Memórias do Cárcere.* Rio de Janeiro, José Olympio, 1953. 4 vols.

Silveira Peixoto, José Benedicto. *Falam os Escritores.* Curitiba, Editôra Guaíra Limitada, 1941.

Simplício, José. *Retrato Popular de um Homem.* Rio de Janeiro, Ariel Editôra, 1937.

Smith, T. Lynn. *Brazil: People and Institutions.* Baton Rouge, La., University of Louisiana Press, 1946.

———, and Alexander Marchant, eds. *Brazil: Portrait of Half a Continent.* New York, The Dryden Press, Inc., 1951.

Tavares de Sá, Hernane. *The Brazilians, People of Tomorrow.* New York, The John Day Co., 1947.

Torres, Alberto. *O Problema Nacional Brasileiro.* 3d ed.; São Paulo, Companhia Editôra Nacional, 1938.

Veríssimo, Érico. *Brazilian Literature.* New York, The Macmillan Co., 1945.

Vianna Moog, Clodomir. *Uma Interpretação da Literatura Brasileira.* Rio de Janeiro, Casa do Estudante do Brasil, 1943.

Walker, Harvey. "The Vargas Regime," in *Brazil,* edited by Lawrence F. Hill. Berkeley and Los Angeles, University of California Press, 1947.

Werneck Sodré, Nelson. *História da Literatura Brasileira: Seus Fundamentos Económicos.* 2d ed.; Rio de Janeiro, José Olympio, 1940.

———. *Orientações do Pensamento Brasileiro.* Rio de Janeiro, Casa Editôra Vecchi, 1942.

INDEX

Index

Agua-Mãe (José Lins do Rego), 64, 70–72, José Américo de. *See* Américo de Almeida, José
Alvim Correa, Roberto, 61
Amado, Jorge, 10, 18, 37, 38, 40, 41, 48, 83–108, 128, 157 ff.
Américo de Almeida, José, 25–31, 32, 37, 38, 42, 47, 48–49, 138, 139
Amoroso Lima, Alceu, 21, 157–158
Andrade, Almir de, 66, 146, 152
Andrade, Mário de, 19, 21, 27, 50
Andrade, Oswald de, 18, 19, 20
Andrade Muricy, José Cândido de, 30, 100
Angústia (Graciliano Ramos), 41, 112, 114, 116, 117, 122, 126–129, 131
Aranha, José Pereira da Graça. *See* Graça Aranha, José Pereira da
Assis, Joaquim Maria Machado de. *See* Machado de Assis, Joaquim Maria
O Ateneu (Raul Pompéia), 53
Athayde, Tristão de. *See* Amoroso Lima, Alceu

A Bagaceira (José Américo de Almeida), 27–30, 138, 139
Banguê (José Lins do Rego), 47, 50, 53–56, 61, 65, 73
Bernardes, Artur da Silva. *See* Silva Bernardes, Artur da
Boas, Franz, 13, 23
Bopp, Raul, 20

O Boqueirão (José Américo de Almeida), 37
Borba, José Osório de Morais. *See* Osório de Morais Borba, José
Brandão entre o Mar e o Amor (Jorge Amado et al.), 161–163

Cacao, 83, 88, 89, 90, 91
Cacáu (Jorge Amado), 37, 86, 88–89, 92, 100, 102
Caetés (Graciliano Ramos), 37, 115, 120–123, 129
Calunga (Jorge de Lima), 37
Caminho de Pedras (Rachel de Queiroz), 41, 139, 142, 146–148
Campos, Siqueira, 15
Cangaceiros (José Lins do Rego), 42
Canudos campaign, 10–12
Capitães da Areia (Jorge Amado), 98–100, 102, 103, 104
Carpeaux, Otto Maria, 78, 117–118
Carvalho, Ronald de, 165
Casa-Grande e Senzala (Gilberto Freyre), 7, 23, 38, 52, 56, 141
Catimbó (Ascenso Ferreira), 20
Cervantes, Miguel de, 75
Cobra Norato (Raul Bopp), 20
Coffee, 4, 8, 10, 31
Coiteiros (José Américo de Almeida), 37
Communism, 17, 18, 32, 33, 34, 85, 101, 102, 103
Copacabana rebellion, 15, 16, 18, 25, 31

Correa, Roberto Alvim. *See* Alvim Correa, Roberto
Os Corumbas (Amando Fontes), 37
Cunha, Euclydes da, 10–12, 16, 20, 27, 35, 69, 129

Dantas, Pedro. *See* Morais Neto, Prudente de
Doidinho (José Lins do Rego), 46, 50, 52–53
Dom Casmurro (Machado de Assis), 119
Don Quixote, 75
A Donzela e a Moura Torta (Rachel de Queiroz), 137–138
Dostoevski, Fedor Mikhailovich, 119
Drought, 5–6, 26, 136, 138

Essa Negra Fulô (Jorge de Lima), 20
Eurídice (José Lins do Rego), 75–78, 79

Ferreira, Ascenso, 20
Ferreira Lampião, Virgulino, 104
Figueiredo, Guilherme de, 132
Fogo Morto (José Lins do Rego), 72–75, 78, 158
Folklore, 20, 21, 24, 71, 97, 102, 107
Fontes, Amando, 37, 143
Freud, Sigmund, 76
Freyre, Gilberto, 7, 10, 12–13, 22–25, 27, 31, 38, 40, 47–48, 52, 56, 57, 71, 95, 141

O Galo de Ouro (Rachel de Queiroz), 42
Gobineau, Joseph Arthur, Comte de, 13, 27
Gold, Michael, 93
Gomes, Eduardo, 15
Gonçalves, Floriano, 116–117, 121–122
Graça Aranha, José Pereira da, 20

Infância (Graciliano Ramos), 111–114
Integralistas, 33, 38, 39

James, Preston E., 6
Jardim, Luis, 25
João Miguel (Rachel de Queiroz), 37, 137, 142–146

John VI, King of Portugal, 8
Joyce, James, 41, 47
Jubiabá (Jorge Amado), 92, 94–97, 102, 103, 104, 159

Lampião. *See* Ferreira Lampião, Virgulino
Liberal Alliance, 25, 31, 32
Lieutenants' party, 14, 15, 17, 25, 31, 33
Lima, Alceu Amoroso. *See* Amoroso Lima, Alceu
Lima, Jorge de, 20, 37
Lins, Álvaro, 25, 79, 86, 108, 119, 128
Lins do Rego, José, 10, 12, 25, 37, 40, 42, 45–79, 96, 107, 115, 157 ff.
Livro do Nordeste (Gilberto Freyre), 22
Luis, Washington, 31

Machado, Aníbal, 161
Machado, Dionélio, 38
Machado de Assis, Joaquim Maria, 111, 119
Maciel, António, 10–11
Macunaíma: O Herói sem Nenhum Carácter (Mário de Andrade), 21, 27
Mar Morto (Jorge Amado), 97–98, 102, 103, 104, 106
Martin, Percy Alvin, 34
Mello Franco, Affonso Arinos de, 4
Menino de Engenho (José Lins do Rego), 37, 50, 51–52, 73
Milliet, Sérgio, 10, 36, 101, 106
Modern Art Week, 18, 19
Modernist movement, 14, 19, 20, 21, 22, 24, 27, 84
O Moleque Ricardo (José Lins do Rego), 49, 50, 56–57, 62, 97
Montenegro, Olívio, 46, 47, 57, 105, 107, 154
Morais Neto, Prudente de, 63
Muricy, José Cândido de Andrade. *See* Andrade Muricy, José Cândido

National Liberation Alliance, 33, 34, 101, 116

October rebellion, 32
Osório de Morais Borba, José, 119, 132
Osório de Oliveira, José, 22, 69

O País do Carnaval (Jorge Amado), 84–85, 86–88, 102, 162
A Parahyba e Seus Problemas (José Américo de Almeida), 26–27
Pau Brasil (Oswald de Andrade), 20
Paulicéia Desvairada (Mário de Andrade), 19
Pedra Bonita (José Lins do Rego), 42, 64, 67–69, 158
Peregrino Júnior, João, 159–160
Pessoa, Epitácio, 14–15, 16, 26
Pessoa, João, 25
Pierson, Donald, 93, 158
Pompéia, Raul, 53
Portinari, Cândido, 50
Prestes, Júlio, 31, 32
Prestes, Luis Carlos, 16–18, 32–34, 101
Prestes Column, 16–17, 31, 104
O Problema Nacional Brasileiro (Alberto Torres), 13
Pureza (José Lins do Rego), 42, 64, 65–67, 73, 75, 76
Putnam, Samuel, 10, 11, 27, 40–42

Queiroz, Eça de, 114, 122
Queiroz, Rachel de, 6, 37, 40, 41–42, 48, 135–154, 157, 159, 160, 163
O Quinze (Rachel de Queiroz), 37, 136, 138–142, 143, 147, 153

Racial mixtures, 7–8, 12, 13, 23, 27, 93
Ramos, Artur, 94, 96
Ramos, Graciliano, 6, 10, 37, 38, 40, 41, 48, 111–132, 157 ff.
Regionalism, 4–5, 12, 22, 24, 25, 31, 61, 122, 131, 132, 160, 164, 165
Rego, José Lins do. *See* Lins do Rego, José
Riacho Doce (José Lins do Rego), 42, 64, 69–71, 76
A Rua do Siriry (Amando Fontes), 143

Salgado, Plínio, 33, 38–39
São Bernardo (Graciliano Ramos), 37, 114, 115, 117, 119, 122, 123–126, 128, 131, 132
São Jorge dos Ilhéus (Jorge Amado), 91–92, 102, 103
Schmidt, Augusto Frederico, 115
Seara Vermelha (Jorge Amado), 100–101, 102, 103, 104
Os Sertões (Euclydes da Cunha), 10, 27, 42, 67, 69
Silva Bernardes, Artur da, 14, 16
Slavery, 3, 7, 8, 27, 52, 57, 143
Sodré, Nelson Werneck. *See* Werneck Sodré, Nelson
Sugar cane, 3, 4, 6, 9, 10, 28, 54
Suor (Jorge Amado), 37, 86, 92, 93–94, 102, 103, 105

Tenentes. *See* Lieutenants' party
Terras do Sem Fim (Jorge Amado), 40, 89–91, 92, 102, 103, 106, 161, 164
Torres, Alberto, 13, 27
As Três Marias (Rachel de Queiroz), 42, 136, 139, 142, 148–152, 153–154

Urucungo (Raul Bopp), 20
Usina (José Lins do Rego), 50, 57–59, 62

Vargas, Getúlio, 25, 26, 31–33, 34, 35, 38–39
Veríssimo, Érico, 4
Vianna Moog, Clodomir, 5
Vidas Secas (Graciliano Ramos), 41, 112, 129–131, 160
Viegas, Pinheiro, 84
Villa-Lobos, Heitor, 50

Werneck Sodré, Nelson, 9, 84

Zola, Émile, 86

The "novel of the Northeast" has been the dominant genre in Brazilian fiction from its inception in the 1930's. José Lins do Rego, Jorge Amado, Rachel de Queiroz, and Graciliano Ramos are the outstanding creators of this genre. These four novelists and their significance in Latin American literature are the subject of this study.

In Brazil the period of the 1930's was one of tropical efflorescence, when literature, along with almost all other phases of creativity, seemed to enter upon a new life. Here, as elsewhere, the age was marked by social and political ferment, some of which is reflected in the novel as social protest or political intent.

The present study shows how, despite the documentary and sociological aspects of the new writing, the fiction of these four novelists often attained the level of art. Usually relying on the conventional techniques of the realistic novel, they have created vivid